BEAUTIFUL QUILTS

ART DECO

Making classic quilts and modern variations

JENNI DOBSON

Illustrations by

PENNY BROWN

Sterling Publishing Co., Inc. New York

A Sterling/Museum Quilts Book

Editors: Ljiljana Baird and Annlee Landman
Designer: Bet Ayer

Library of Congress Cataloging-in-Publication Data

Dobson, Jenni.
    Beautiful quilts: art deco: making classic quilts & modern
variations / by Jenni Dobson.
        p.   cm.
    "A Sterling / Museum Quilts book."
    Includes index.
    ISBN 0-8069-1326-6
    1. Patchwok — Patterns.   I. Title
TT835. D633   1995
746.46 — dc20

95 — 230 18
CIP

2 4 6 8 10 9 7 5 3 1

A STERLING/MUSEUM QUILTS BOOK

Published by Sterling Publishing Company, Inc.,
387 Park Avenue South, New York, NY 10016
and by Museum Quilts Publications Inc.
Published in the UK by Museum Quilts (UK) Inc.,
254-258 Goswell Road, London EC1V 7EB
Distributed in Canada by Sterling Publishing
c/o Canadian Manda Group, One Atlantic Avenue, Suite 105
Toronto, Ontario, Canada M6K 3E7
Distributed in Australia by Capricorn Link (Australia) Pty Ltd.,
P.O. Box 6651, Baulkham Hills Business Centre
NSW 2153, Australia

Copyright © Museum Quilts Publications, Inc. 1995
Text © Jenni Dobson 1995
Illustrations © Penny Brown 1995

The author has endeavored to ensure that all project instructions are accurate. However, due to variations in readers' individual skill and materials available, neither the author nor the publisher can accept responsibility for damages or losses resulting from the instructions herein. All instructions should be studied and clearly understood before beginning any project.

Printed and bound in France by Partenaires

ISBN: 0-8069-1326-6

CONTENTS

INTRODUCTION

The term Art Deco is used to describe many different design styles that were fashionable between World War I and World War II. As a style, it is multi-faceted and easily recognizable. For most of us, Art Deco conjures up pictures of the decorative chinaware of Clarice Cliff, the elegant lines of Chiparus' bronze figures, as well as the simplified and squared-off geometric shapes of the Chrysler Building in Chicago or the interiors of old cinema theaters.

Design movements are often the product of new ideas and attitudes towards the technical developments of the period. During the twenty years between the wars, great advances were made in science, engineering and industry. It was a period of progress and optimism. Factories were built and the production line was invented to accommodate mass production. There were technological developments in all kinds of materials which demanded innovative use by, among others, architects, furniture designers, jewelers, and industrial designers. Their responses to this challenge in turn inspired the creativity of practitioners in other disciplines. Artists designed posters and printed textiles, sets and costumes for the theater and ballet with this new technology at hand.

Advances in motor and air travel made the world accessible to the rising middle classes. Decorative motifs from Africa, the Orient and Russia found their way into the Art Deco vocabulary. And, following the opening of the tomb of Tutankhamen in 1923, the design world went temporarily crazy for things "Egyptienne".

Art Deco was a total look. The prevailing design philosophy was to improve design standards at all levels of human activity, from the design of a factory to the design of a perfume bottle. There were different design camps, but all were convinced that every detail of daily life was worthy of the designer's attention – from the taps at the washbasin to the shape of a handbag.

The heightened sense of design was accompanied by a firm appreciation of fine craftsmanship. As craftsmen devised new ways of working with newly available materials, or exploited new colors for glass, glazes or textiles, they did so with an aspiration towards excellence and the aim of improving the quality of life.

A belief that "form should follow function" governed many of the design decisions of the period. In its most radical form, it produced the minimalism of Le Corbusier who claimed that a house should be a "machine for living in". But Art Deco was essentially about applied arts, and its consumers had largely middle class tastes. They demanded ornament and decoration, not the severe functionalism advocated by the design philosophy of the avant-garde.

The Quilts

Art Deco was a populist movement and it pervaded all aspects of domestic life, including quiltmaking. The stylized, geometric shapes of the Art Deco

Cover of catalog for the quiltmaking contest sponsored by the department store Sears Roebuck and Company for the 1933 Century of Progress Exposition in Chicago

aesthetic were easily adapted into the piecing patterns of patchwork. Stylized flowers, images from everyday life, and exotic motifs from the East all became subjects for patchwork and appliqué.

The quilting revival in America during the two decades of the 1920s and '30s became a nation-wide preoccupation and was underwritten by national newspapers who could boast that quilt columns were their most popular feature. The large department stores were quick to realize the lucrative business of selling quilting fabrics and commercial patterns. The influence of color in other Art Deco products was absorbed and introduced into quilts alongside fashionable, new and synthetically derived colors and fabrics used for dressmaking; leftovers from these often found their way into quilts. Particular colors or com-binations of colors predominated. These range from the sophisticated combinations of cyclamen pink, black, white and gray to the bold com- binations of purple and orange. Old colors were given brighter names. Orange became "Tango", reflecting the popularity of the dance. Pale green became "Nile". A lavender dye was produced, adding a new purple shade to the quiltmakers' palette.

Mechanization allowed fabric manufacturers to flood the market with cheap and colorful printed fabrics. This unprecedented availability had a great effect on the design and number of quilts being made. It gave a great burst of enthusiasm to colorful scrap quilts.

The following chapters bring to light just some of the design preoccupations of quiltmakers of the first half of the twentieth century. The eight wonderful Art Deco quilts featured are part of Museum Quilts Gallery in London, England. They have inspired me to analyze their construction and wonder about how they would look if I rearranged their components. By changing the fabric place-ment or choosing a different color scheme, by introducing sashing or removing borders, or turning the blocks on point I was able to create three "new" alternatives to each basic block pattern.

There is great satisfaction in designing your own quilt, and I hope that this book will encourage all quilters to create their very own quilts.

Art Deco Dresden Plate

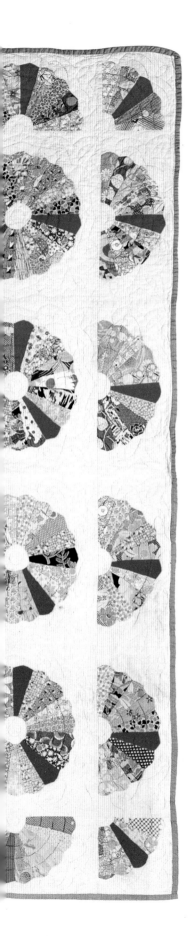

DRESDEN PLATE

One of the reasons for the popularity of this design is the opportunity it presents for using lots of different fabrics together. During the 1920s and '30s, new dyes filled the market with a multitude of colorful printed fabrics. A wonderfully versatile pattern, its many wedge components can be re-arranged to make a variety of new designs. Break it down into sections and it becomes one of the radiating, fan-like motifs so favored by Art Deco designers. The quilt opposite has used half and quarter plates to frame the complete plates within a border of spreading fan motifs.
In *Sunrise*, the whole quilt is composed of radiating half-plates like rising suns against a dark sky, while *Stylized Vine Trails* has an appliqué border whose naive flowers echo the plate centers.

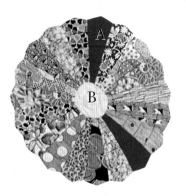

Skill level: Intermediate
Quilt size: 70 x 84 inches
Finished block: 14 x 14 inches
Number of blocks: 20 blocks, 18 half blocks,
4 quarter blocks

MATERIALS

Off-white/unbleached cotton 4¹/₂ yards
Assorted scrap prints equivalent to 3¹/₄ yards
Green for binding ³/₈ yard
Backing 4¹/₄ yards
Batting 74 x 88 inches

CUTTING INSTRUCTIONS

Make templates for Wedge A and Inner circle B
without seam allowances. Add ¹/₄ inch as you cut
each piece.

Off-white fabric

1. Cut 20 background squares, 14¹/₂ x 14¹/₂ inches;
18 rectangles, 14¹/₂ x 7¹/₂ inches and four squares,
7¹/₂ x 7¹/₂ inches.

2. Using Template B, cut 20 inner circles.

3. Cut nine ovals using Template D and one circle
using Template E for the centers of the half and
quarter blocks. Remember to add ¹/₄ inch around
each piece as you cut. Do **not** divide D and E
pieces until they have been gathered around paper
templates as instructed.

Scrap prints

1. Cut 600 A pieces: 20 wedges for each full plate,
ten for each half block and five for each quarter
block.

Green fabric

1. Cut eight strips, 1¹/₄ inches wide across the full
width of the fabric. Join together to make a
continuous length for separate binding.

PUTTING THE BLOCK TOGETHER

1. Place two A pieces right sides together and stitch
along the marked pencil line. Repeat to make ten
pairs. Sew five pairs together into a half block.
Press, then join the two half blocks.

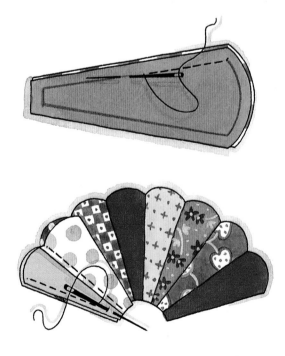

2. Fold the background square into quarters and crease lightly, for positioning guidelines. Pin and baste the plate to the background. Stitch a line of running stitches around the inner circle of the plate within the seam allowance, to stabilize the layers.

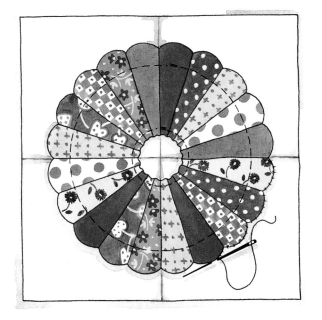

3. Appliqué the outer edge of the plate to the background by turning under the seam allowances of the segments and slipstitching to follow the contour.

4. Cut a circle of paper using Template B. Do not add seam allowances. Place the paper template on the wrong side of a fabric circle B and stitch a row of small running stitches within the seam

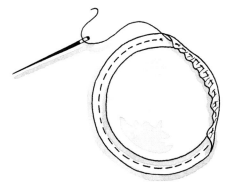

allowance. Pull the thread ends to gather the fabric into a smooth circle. Secure the thread and press carefully. Use spray starch to help set the shape.

5. Remove the paper, pin to the block center and appliqué in place. Make 20 full blocks.

6. Prepare the D and E pieces, as for the B inner circles, gathering around paper templates. Press to set the shape, remove the papers, then carefully cut the D ovals in half and the E circle in quarters.

7. Pin the D semi-circles in position on the 18 half blocks, and appliqué in place.

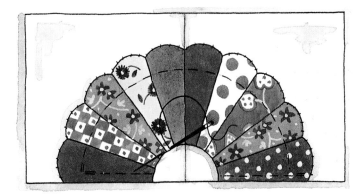

8. Pin the E pieces to the 4 quarter blocks and appliqué.

ASSEMBLING THE QUILT TOP

1. Lay out the blocks using the quilt as a guide. To create additional surface interest and a sense of movement, carefully position the wedges of dominant color.

2. Assemble the blocks in vertical rows. Note that the sides consist of four half blocks with a quarter

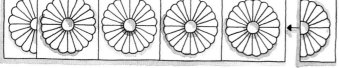

block at each end. The remaining columns have four full blocks with half blocks at each end.

3. Join the columns together, carefully matching the block seams.

MARKING, QUILTING & FINISHING

1. Mark the quilting motif in each corner of every block, including the half and quarter blocks of the border. The plates are quilted with concentric circles which can be marked as you go using circles of sticky-backed plastic.

2. Divide the backing fabric into two equal lengths. Cut away the selvedges, then sew a $^1/_2$ inch seam down one long side. Press the seam to one side.

3. Assemble the quilt layers and baste thoroughly.

4. Quilt the motifs and concentric circles in the plates.

5. Trim the batting and backing even with the quilt top. Baste the edges of the quilt together inside the seam allowance. Finish the raw edges of the quilt using the Separate binding method as described in the Techniques section.

SUNRISE

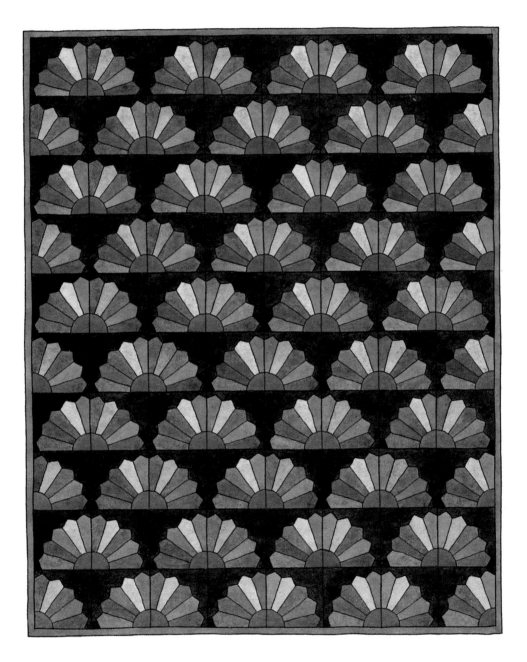

Skill level: Beginner
Quilt size: 60 x 48 inches
Finished block: 6 x 12 inches
Number of blocks: 35 half plate blocks, 10 quarter plate blocks

MATERIALS

Black 2¹/₂ yards
Crimson red ¹/₄ yard
Blue for binding ¹/₄ yard
Solid color scraps equivalent to 2¹/₄ yards
Backing 2¹/₄ yards
Batting 52 x 64 inches

CUTTING INSTRUCTIONS

Make Template C for the wedge, and D and E for the Sunrise centers. Template C includes a ¹/₄ inch seam allowance. Pieces cut from Templates D and E need seam allowances added.

Black fabric

1. Cut 35 rectangles, 6¹/₂ x 12¹/₂ inches and 10 squares, 6¹/₂ x 6¹/₂ inches.

Crimson red fabric

1. Cut 18 ovals for the half block centers, using Template D. Cut three circles, using Template E for the quarter block centers. Do not divide these pieces at this stage.

Solid color scraps

1. Using Template C, cut 400 wedges.

Binding

1. Cut six strips, 1¹/₄ inches wide across the full width of the fabric. Join to make a continuous length for separate binding.

PUTTING THE QUILT TOGETHER

1. Fold each wedge in half lengthwise, right sides out, and sew a ¹/₄ inch seam across the top.

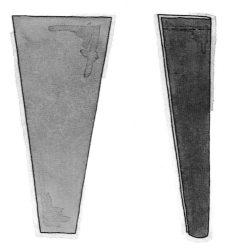

2. Open out flat and the point automatically turns in. Press the seam open as far as possible then press the tip into a small triangle. (This technique is an adaptation of one described by Maggie Malone in Quilting Shortcuts, Sterling, NY, 1986.)

3. Following the instructions for *Art Deco Dresden Plate*, piece wedges into 35 sets, each of ten wedges, and apply to the black rectangles for the half blocks. Piece the remaining wedges into ten sets of five each, and apply these to the black squares for the quarter blocks.

4. Prepare the centers as for the main quilt, but after pressing, cut the D ovals in half on the broken red line and cut the E circles into quarters. Position the D semi-circles on the half blocks and the E quarter-circles on the quarter blocks, and appliqué in place.

5. Using the quilt as a guide, assemble the blocks into ten rows: five rows of four half blocks, and five rows of three half blocks with a quarter block at each end.

6. Arrange the rows in an alternating sequence and join together to complete the top.

7. Cut two strips, 9 inches wide, across the width of the backing fabric. Join these end-to-end with a $1/2$ inch seam, trim away the selvedges then press. Join to one long side of the remaining piece of backing and cut away the selvedge.

8. Assemble the quilt layers and baste together. Quilt around the semi-circle centers. Quilt radiating lines through the fan segments and fill the black background with a simple grid.

9. Finish the raw edges of the quilt using the Separate binding method as described in the Techniques section.

STYLIZED VINE TRAIL

Skill level: Intermediate
Quilt size: 66 x 66 inches
Finished block: 12 x 12 inches
Number of blocks: 16

MATERIALS

Cream 3³/₄ yards
Green ⁵/₈ yard
Red ⁵/₈ yard
Assorted red, yellow and brown prints equivalent
   to 1³/₄ yards
Backing 4 yards
Batting 70 x 70 inches

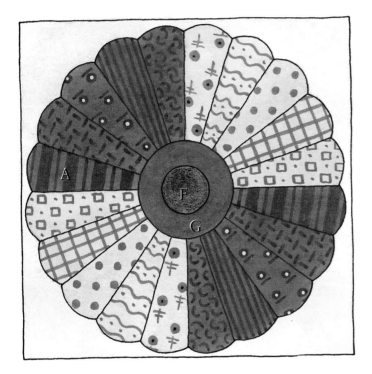

CUTTING INSTRUCTIONS

Make templates for the A wedge and the B circle as for *Art Deco Dresden Plate*. For the plate centers and border flowers, make Templates F and G.

Cream fabric

1. Cut two border strips, 9¹/₂ x 66¹/₂ inches and two border strips, 9¹/₂ x 48¹/₂ inches. These measurements are precise, with no excess, to position the appliqué correctly.

2. Cut 16 squares, 12¹/₂ x 12¹/₂ inches.

Green fabric

1. Using Template F, cut 36 circles and gather around paper templates.

2. Use the method described in the Techniques section to make 12 yards of bias strip, ³/₄ inch wide for the flower stems.

Red fabric

1. Cut eight strips, 1¹/₄ inches wide, across the full width of the fabric. Join together to make a continuous length for separate binding.

2. Using Template G, cut and prepare 32 circles.

3. Using Template B, cut and prepare four circles for the small border flowers in the corners.

Assorted red, yellow and brown prints

1. For each of the 16 plates, use Template A to cut ten wedges from each of two color groups. Cut a total of 320 wedges.

PUTTING THE QUILT TOGETHER

1. Following the instructions for *Art Deco Dresden Plate*, make up 16 blocks, organizing wedges into four groups of five each. Center the plates onto 12¹/₂ inch squares. Appliqué a prepared G circle on each plate. To complete the block, appliqué an F circle in the center.

2. Press along the length of the green bias strip into thirds across the width to turn in the raw edges.

3. Fold the short borders into four equal sections and crease lightly. On the long borders, measure 9$\frac{1}{2}$ inches cm from both ends and lightly crease, then crease to divide the space between into four equal sections. Using the quilt as a guide, place the folded bias strip diagonally between sections, pin and baste into place. Work the borders as pairs.

4. Use the remaining bias for the flower stems, cutting lengths about 4$\frac{1}{2}$ inches for each flower. Pin in position, tucking one end under the long stem. Sew all stems in place then add the large G flowers so that they cover the remaining raw end of the stem. Note that one flower cannot be added until the border is attached to the quilt. Position the four smaller B flowers at each corner. Appliqué prepared green F circles in the center of each flower.

5. Arrange the blocks as required. Sew in four horizontal rows of four blocks each, then join the rows together.

6. Pin, then sew the short borders to opposite sides of the quilt. Press, then add the longer borders. Complete the flower appliqué over the border seams.

7. Divide the backing fabric into two equal lengths. Cut away the selvedges, then sew together with a $\frac{1}{2}$ inch seam. Press the seam to one side.

8. Assemble the quilt layers and baste together. Echo quilt $\frac{1}{4}$ inch away from the plates·and border appliqués. Quilt concentric circles between each group of four blocks.

9. Trim the edges of the batting and backing even with the quilt top. Finish the raw edges with the prepared red binding using the Separate binding method as described in the Techniques section.

HARLEQUIN PLATES

For this design follow the "automatic points" method of the
Sunrise quilt to make the plates. The red circles at the block corners
can either be pieced, like the quadrants in the *New York Beauty*
pattern or they can be appliquéd over the seams after the blocks
have been joined.

Art Deco Sailors

FIGURATIVE APPLIQUÉ

Subjects commonplace and exotic were explored by quiltmakers during the Art Deco years, and each quilt in this chapter carries a "look" that is distinctive of the period. The ephemeral beauty of butterflies perhaps makes them a predictable subject, but the representation given here is highly stylized. The stark outline of the wings has a powerful graphic quality typical of the design preference for things "Oriental".

The sailor block marks a trend towards quilt designs with a transportation theme, no doubt inspired by the developments that were taking place in this field at the time.

The *Scottie Dogs* quilt represents that category of innovative and often witty novelty quilt design that was so popular.

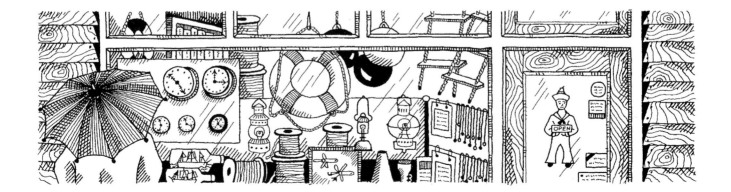

Skill level: Intermediate
Quilt size: 84 x 66 inches
Finished block: 16 x 16 inches
Number of blocks: 13 sailors, 4 anchors

MATERIALS

White 2 yards
Lavender 2¹/₂ yard
Dark gray 1¹/₂ yards
Black ¹/₂ yard
Pale pink 1 scrap at least 10 x 12 inches
Backing 4 yards
Batting 86 x 68 inches
Narrow ribbon for lanyards 12 inches light, and
   27 inches dark
Embroidery thread for details of faces and clothes

CUTTING INSTRUCTIONS

1. Prepare finished-size templates for the separate shapes of the sailor suit, hat, shoes and face. Transfer the details for the face and clothing which will be embroidered later.

2. Place templates right side up on the right side of the fabric and trace around the shape. The drawn pencil line represents your turning under and sewing line. For marking on dark fabrics, a light-colored pencil may be used or a sharpened sliver of dry soap. Add a scant ¹/₄ inch around each piece as you cut. Remember to transfer all details to the cut shapes.

White fabric
1. Cut four squares, 16¹/₂ x 16¹/₂ inches.

2. Cut two squares, 16⁷/₈ x 16⁷/₈ inches for the backgrounds of the four anchor blocks. These will be cut apart after the blocks have been appliquéd.

3. Using the templates, cut nine sailor suits and 13 hats.

4. Cut two squares, 4¹/₂ x 4¹/₂ inches in half across the diagonal.

Lavender fabric
1. Cut nine squares, 16¹/₂ x 16¹/₂ inches.

2. Cut 12 squares, 4¹/₂ x 4¹/₂ inches.

3. Cut three squares, 4⁷/₈ x 4⁷/₈ inches in half across the diagonal.

Dark gray fabric
1. Cut 24 sashing strips, 16¹/₂ x 4¹/₂ inches.

2. Cut 12 sashing strips, 8 x 4¹/₂ inches.

Black fabric

1. Using the templates, cut four sailor suits, 13 pairs of shoes and four anchors.

Pale pink fabric

1. Cut 13 faces using the appropriate template.

SEWING THE BLOCKS

1. Fold the two large white background squares across the diagonal and crease lightly to help position the anchor pieces. Prepare the anchor by fingerpressing under the seam allowance all around, then pin in place on the background and stitch down. Appliqué another anchor in the opposite corner.

2. On the remaining large white background square, appliqué two more anchors and press. Divide the anchor blocks in half across the marked diagonal line.

3. For a sailor block, position the face on a $16\frac{1}{2}$ inch background square. Turn raw edges under and sew down except where the edge will be covered by another shape. Add the hat, and then the suit, and finally slip the shoes under the trouser hems.

4. Embroider the details of the suit and face. Cut a piece of narrow ribbon about 3 inches, tie a small knot in the middle then attach to the point of the V-neck.

5. Make four sailor blocks on white grounds with black suits and nine on lavender grounds with white suits.

ASSEMBLING THE QUILT TOP

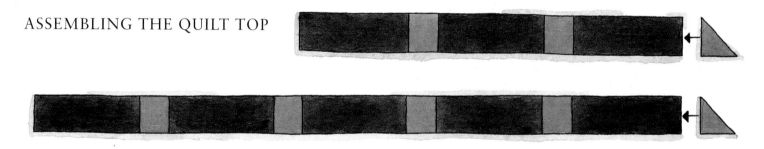

1. Lay out all the blocks with the sashing strips and posts. The short sashing strips are for the vertical sides of the quilt and will be longer than required. Pin and sew sashing strips to posts.

2. Join the blocks and sashing strips together in diagonal rows taking care to match the corners of blocks and posts. Fill in the gaps between blocks with small white triangles. Join the rows of blocks and strips together to complete the top.

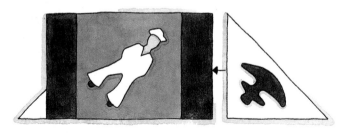

3. Straighten the sides of the quilt, cutting away the points of the perimeter blocks. At each corner, trace around a saucer, and cut away excess fabric for a smooth rounded corner.

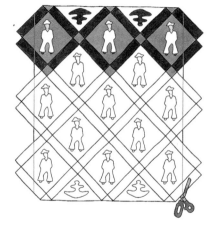

MARKING, QUILTING & FINISHING

1. Press the quilt carefully and remove any loose threads which may show through to the front. Mark out the *Baptist Fan* quilting pattern as instructed for *Art Deco Snail Trails*.

2. Divide the background fabric in two equal lengths. With right sides together and selvedges even, sew a $1/2$ inch seam. Trim away the selvedge and press to one side.

3. Assemble the quilt layers and baste thoroughly. Outline quilt the appliquéd motifs and other quilting patterns.

4. Trim the edges of the quilt top and backing to allow for $1/2 – 3/4$ inch turnings. Trim the batting to the finished size. Turn in the allowance of the backing to enclose the batting. Turn in the allowance of the quilt top, pin and baste the folded edges together.

5. Slipstitch the folds together to complete the Fold-finish binding method, as described in the Techniques section.

SCOTTIE DOGS

Skill level: Beginner
Quilt size: 50¼ x 63 inches
Finished block: 9 x 9 inches
Number of blocks: 12

MATERIALS

Blue print 2¹/₄ yards
Blue ¹/₃ yard
White ⁷/₈ yard
Scrap plaids equivalent to ¹/₄ yard
Backing 3 yards
Batting 54 x 67 inches
Binding 6¹/₂ yards
Black embroidery thread

CUTTING INSTRUCTIONS

Make templates for pieces A, B, C, D. Add a scant ¹/₄ inch around each piece as you cut out the fabric shapes.

Blue print fabric

1. Cut four strips, 6¹/₂ x 53 inches for the border.

2. Cut six setting squares, 9¹/₂ x 9¹/₂ inches.

3. Cut three squares, 14¹/₂ x 14¹/₂ inches across both diagonals to make side triangles. There will be two extra.

4. Cut two squares, 7¹/₂ x 7¹/₂ inches in half diagonally to make four corner triangles.

Blue fabric

1. Cut 12 heads using Template A, 12 front legs from Template B and 12 back legs with Template C.

White fabric

1. Cut 12 squares, 9¹/₂ x 9¹/₂ inches for the block background.

Assorted plaids

1. Use Template D to cut a total of 12 coats.

Binding

1. Cut six strips, 1¹/₄ inch wide across the full width of the fabric. Join strips to make a continuous length for separate binding.

SEWING THE BLOCK

1. Assemble a Scottie dog by attaching the head, front legs and back legs to the plaid coat, placing the pieces in turn, right sides together with the coat. Match and sew carefully.

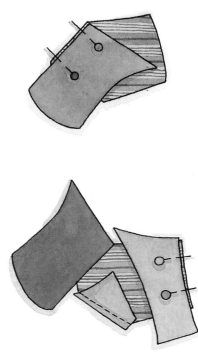

2. Turn under and baste all the outside edges of the assembled dog. Then position the dog onto a background square and sew in place. The background fabric behind the appliqué may be

trimmed away if you wish. Embroider the dog's features.

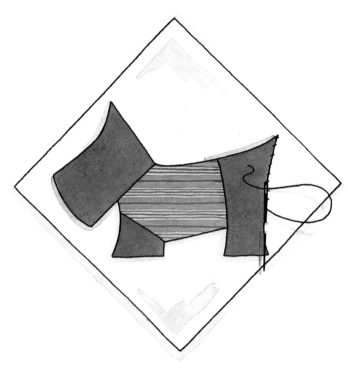

3. Make a total of 12 blocks.

PUTTING THE QUILT TOGETHER

1. Lay out the appliqué blocks and place the setting squares in between, using the illustration as a guide. Aim for balance in the arrangement of the plaid coats. Add the side and corner triangles to fill in the spaces.

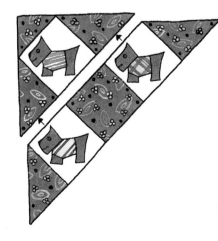

2. Join the blocks and setting squares into diagonal rows, making sure the end triangles are correctly placed at the ends of the rows. Press seam allowances joining the blocks in opposite directions on alternate rows. Join the rows of blocks together.

3. Pin, then sew two of the border strips to the top and bottom of the quilt working out from the center to each end. After stitching, press then trim the excess border fabric. In the same manner, attach the side borders.

4. Divide the backing fabric into two equal lengths and seam together with a $1/2$ inch seam. Trim away the selvedges and press to one side.

5. Spread the quilt top on a firm surface and mark the paw print quilting motifs in the setting squares and triangles.

6. Assemble the quilt layers and baste thoroughly.

7. Quilt the marked design and in-the-ditch around the dogs.

8. Trim the batting and backing even with the quilt top. Baste the edges of the quilt together within the seam allowance .

9. Use the prepared plaid binding to finish the raw edges of the quilt with the Separate binding method as described in the Techniques section.

BUTTERFLIES

Skill level: Beginner
Quilt size: 80 x 64 inches
Finished block: 16 x 16 inches
Number of blocks: 20

MATERIALS

Black 5 yards
Cream 1 yard
Solid scraps equivalent to ½ yard
Print scraps equivalent to 2½ yards
Backing 4 yards
Batting 84 x 68 inches
Embroidery thread for antennae

CUTTING INSTRUCTIONS

Make templates for pieces A, B and C. Remember to add a scant ¼ inch seam allowance as you cut out each piece. For pieces Ar and Br, turn the template over and trace the mirror image.

Black fabric
1. Cut 20 background squares, 16½ x 16½ inches.

Cream fabric
1. Using Template A, cut 20 wing shadows. Turn the template over, and cut 20 Ar pieces.

Solid-color scraps
1. Cut 20 bodies, using Template C.

Print scraps
1. Using Template B, cut 20 wings. Turn the template over, and cut 20 Br pieces.

SEWING THE BLOCKS

1. Lightly crease each background block on the diagonal to give placement lines. Position the wing shadows first, basting down the raw edges which will be covered by the wings. Turn under and appliqué the top and sides of the wing shadows to the background block.

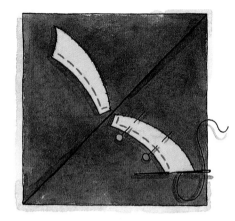

2. Appliqué the wings in position, overlapping the basted edges of the wing shadows. Baste down the edges which will be covered by the body.

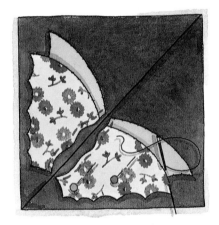

3. Appliqué the body to the background block, covering the raw edges of both wings. Finish the block by embroidering the antennae.

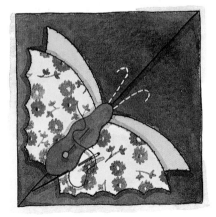

PUTTING THE QUILT TOGETHER

1. Arrange the completed blocks in a pleasing design. Notice that the butterflies fly in different directions rather than following a symmetrical plan. When satisfied with your arrangement, join the blocks together in horizontal rows, pressing the seam allowances on alternate rows in opposite directions. Assemble the rows to complete the top.

2. On a firm surface, mark the floral quilt design in the corner of the blocks.

3. Divide the backing fabric in half. With right sides together and selvedges even, sew parallel to one edge taking a $1/2$ inch seam. Trim away the selvedges and press to one side.

4. Assemble the quilt layers and baste thoroughly, starting at the center and working out to the sides.

5. Quilt the marked flowers, veins in the wings and all around the appliquéd shapes.

6. To finish the raw edges of the quilt using the Self-binding method, trim the batting even with the edge of the quilt top. Trim the backing to leave a $3/4$ inch border all around. Fold in excess backing $1/4$ inch on all sides. Bring the fold over to the front and slipstitch in place, mitering the corners neatly to finish.

CHINESE LANTERNS

This light-hearted design offers the chance to mix
"show-case" motifs from printed fabrics with pieced and appliquéd
lanterns. An interesting set, combining geometric and
scattered floral fabric strengthens the period mood.

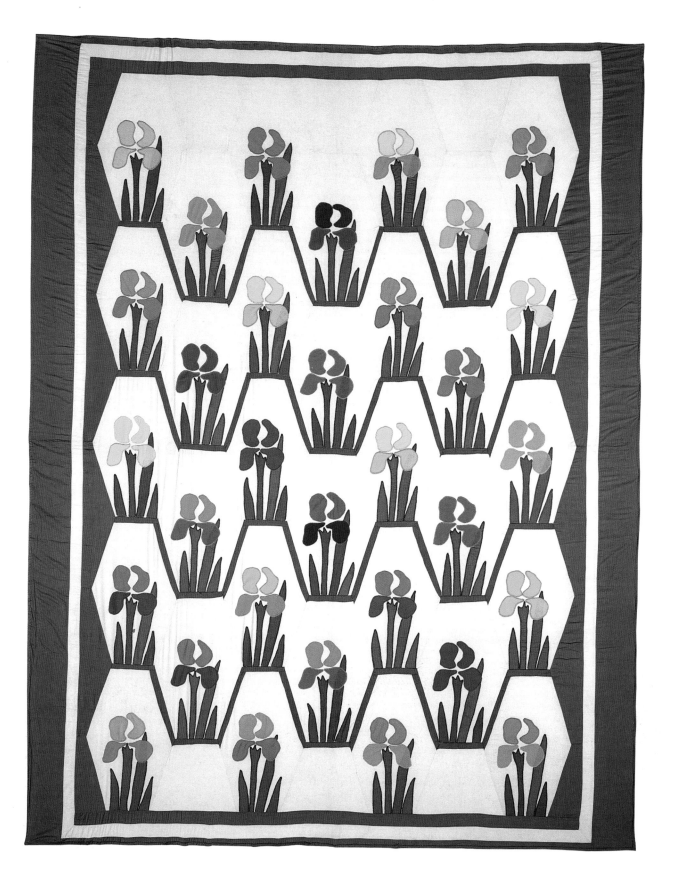

Art Deco Irises

FLORAL APPLIQUÉ

The beauty of flowers has inspired artists and needlewomen through the centuries. Ways of seeing and portraying flowers have changed, and certain varieties experience greater popularity at different times. The flowers featured in this chapter – the Iris, Tiger Lily, Sunflower and Water Lily – were particularly fashionable with Art Deco designers and quiltmakers. The use of strong colorful fabrics strikes a visual relationship with the world of printing and graphics where the Art Deco movement made considerable impact.

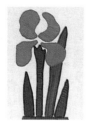

Skill Level: Intermediate
Quilt size: 96 x 78 inches
Finished block: 18 x 11 1/2 inches
Number of blocks: 32 blocks

MATERIALS

White 4 1/2 yards
Mint green 3 3/4 yards (including binding)
Assorted solid colors equivalent to 1 1/4 yards
Embroidery threads to match or tone with solid
    colors
Backing 5 1/2 yards
Batting 100 x 82 inches

CUTTING INSTRUCTIONS

Make full-size templates of the hexagon block, the
side and corner setting units including 1/4 inch seam
allowances. Make templates of the petals and
leaves without seam allowances. Add a scant 1/4 inch
around each fabric piece as you cut.

White fabric

1. Cut two side border strips, 94 x 2 inches, and
two border strips, 68 x 2 inches for the top and
bottom.

2. Using the block template, cut 32 hexagon
blocks. Cut six half-hexagon blocks, adding a
1/4 inch seam allowance to the center line across the
block.

Mint green fabric

1. Cut two side border strips, 97 x 6 1/2 inches and
two border strips, 65 x 1 1/2 inches for the top and
bottom edges.

2. Using templates, cut eight side setting pieces and
four corner setting pieces.

3. Cut seven strips, 2 inches wide across the full
width of the fabric. Sew strips together to make a
continuous length for Separate binding.

4. Cut 24 trellis strips, 10 1/2 x 1 1/4 inches and 28
trellis strips, 7 1/2 x 1 1/4 inches.

5. Using the templates, cut 32 sets of three leaves
and 32 stems.

Assorted solid colors

1. Using the templates, cut 32 sets of petals as for
the leaves. Note that some of the flowers have all
the petals in a single color but others have the top
and bottom pairs in different shades of one color.

PUTTING THE BLOCK TOGETHER

1. Lay a hexagon block over the enlarged paper
block to help position the pieces. Outlines can be
lightly marked with pencil or the hexagon can be
laid over the paper block to position each shape.

2. Begin by applying the stem and leaves. Fingerpress seam allowances to the wrong side and pin or
baste in position. To retain the character of the
original quilt, appliqué with buttonhole stitch in
matching green thread.

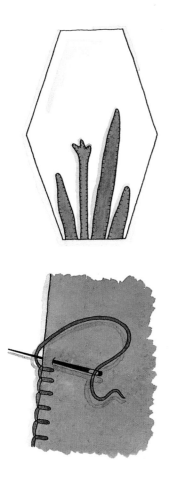

into the following groups: four A blocks, with trellis along the top and right side; nine B blocks, with trellis along the top edge; eight C blocks, with trellis on the top three sides; and four D blocks, with trellis along the top and left side. Pin short trellis strips to the top edge of three half hexagon blocks.

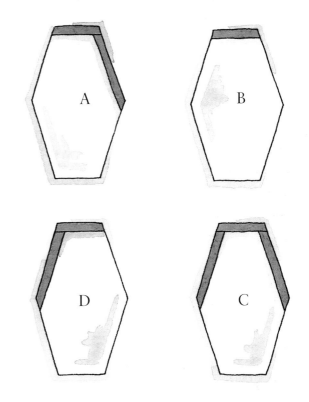

3. Add the flower petals. The colored threads for buttonhole stitching need not match the fabric exactly; using a lighter or darker tone can enhance the appearance.

4. Make 32 full blocks.

5. The trellis strips are not identical in each block. To work out the trellis arrangement, lay out the appliquéd hexagon blocks using the quilt as a guide. Add the half-hexagon blocks to fill in the spaces.

6. Set aside seven Iris blocks, which do not require trellis strips. Sort the required number of blocks

7. Attach the long trellis strips to the sides of the required blocks first, then sew the shorter trellis strips across the tops of the required blocks. To position each strip, lay right sides to the block with the raw edge of the strip $3/4$ inch from the raw edge of the block. Sew through both layers $1/4$ inch from the raw edge of the strip.

8. Open the strip out even with the edge of the block. Press, then baste close to the edge and treat as one layer when joining the blocks. Always press and secure the side strips before attaching any strips to the top. Add all the trellis strips to the block sets.

ASSEMBLING THE QUILT TOP

1. Lay the blocks out in their correct positions again. Join together in vertical columns, beginning by sewing the base of the first block to the top of the next. Start alternate rows with the appropriate half-block.

2. Join the columns of blocks together, carefully pivoting at the angles on the vertical seams. Join the corner and side triangles together in two vertical columns and attach in the same way.

3. Attach the green inner border strips across the top and bottom of the assembled blocks. Trim as required.

4. Attach the longer white border strips to the sides. Press and trim, then attach the short white border strips across the top and bottom. Press and trim. Sew the remaining green border strips to the sides of the quilt.

QUILTING & FINISHING

1. Divide the backing fabric into two equal lengths and join together with a $1/2$ inch seam. Trim away the selvedges and press.

2. Assemble the quilt layers and baste thoroughly, starting at the center and working out diagonally, vertically and horizontally to the sides.

3. Quilt around the flowers and fill the background with a simple grid.

4. Trim the backing and batting even with the top then baste the layers together at the edges within the seam allowance. Sew the binding strips to the front of the quilt $1/2$ inch from the raw edge. Bring the binding over to the back, turn under a $1/2$ inch fold, and slipstitch to give a $1/2$ inch wide finished binding.

SUNFLOWERS

Skill Level: Intermediate
Quilt size: 81 x 71^1/$_2$ inches
Finished block: 18 x 11^1/$_2$ inches
Number of blocks: 25

MATERIALS

White 5 yards
Green print 1³/4 yards
Bright yellow 2¹/4 yards
Deep yellow 1 yard
Backing 4¹/4 yards
Batting 85 x 75¹/2 inches

CUTTING INSTRUCTIONS

Make full-size templates for the hexagon block, side and corner triangles including a ¹/4 inch seam allowance. Make templates for the sunflower head, center, stem and leaves without seam allowances. Add a scant ¹/4 inch around each piece as you cut out the fabric shapes.

White fabric

1. Using the templates, cut 25 hexagon blocks, six half-hexagon blocks, six side triangles and four corner triangles. Add ¹/4 inch seam allowances around each piece as you cut.

Green print

1. Cut two border strips, 80¹/2 x 2³/4 inches and two border strips, 75 x 2³/4 inches. These outer border strips include extra width to turn over to the back of the quilt for binding.

2. Using the prepared templates, cut 25 sets of stems and leaves.

Bright yellow fabric

1. Cut eight strips of fabric, 2 inches wide across the full width of the fabric. Join strips together to make two border strips, 78 inches and two border strips, 71 inches.

2. From the remaining fabric and using the template, cut 25 sunflower heads.

Deep yellow fabric

1. Cut seven strips of fabric, 2 inches wide across the full width of the fabric. Join the strips together to make two border strips, 74 inches long and two border strips, 68 inches.

2. From the remaining fabric and using the template, cut 25 sunflower centers.

SEWING THE BLOCKS

1. Baste the stem in position on the background hexagon block. Appliqué the pieces in the following order: stem, leaves, sunflower head and the center. To help obtain a smooth curve, prepare

the centers by gathering the seam allowances over a paper template, as described for *Art Deco Dresden Plate.*

2. When the appliqué is complete, trim away the background fabric from behind the large flowers and leaves.

3. Lay the blocks out in vertical columns, filling in the spaces with half blocks as required. Join in vertical rows then sew the vertical seams, pivoting the work carefully at the angles. Inset the side triangles to form the straight edges of the quilt then attach the corner triangles.

4. Sew the longer deep yellow borders to the sides of the quilt. Press, then sew remaining deep yellow borders to the top and bottom edges. Sew the bright yellow and green borders following the same sequence.

5. Using the appliqué leaf template, mark a free arrangement of leaves as a quilting design in each of the half-hexagon blocks.

6. Divide the backing fabric into two equal lengths and join with a $1/2$ inch seam. Trim away the selvedges and press.

7. Assemble the quilt layers. Pin then baste thoroughly.

8. Quilt in-the-ditch around the appliqué shapes and borders, and quilt the marked leaves.

9. Trim the batting and backing on each side to $3/4$ inch smaller than the quilt top. Fold in $1/4$ inch on the raw edge of the outer border, turn over to the quilt back, then stitch in place, mitering the corners neatly to finish.

TIGER LILIES

Skill Level: Intermediate
Quilt size: 65 x 54 inches
Finished block: 11$\frac{1}{2}$ x 18 inches
Number of blocks: 5 blocks, 4 half blocks

MATERIALS

Black 1 yard
Yellow check $^7/_8$ yard
Green $^1/_2$ yard
Rose pink 1 yard
Blue 1 yard
Yellow $1^1/_4$ yards
Backing $3^1/_4$ yards
Batting 69 x 58 inches

CUTTING INSTRUCTIONS

Make full-size templates for the hexagon block, half block, edge and corner triangles, including $^1/_4$ inch seam allowance. Make templates for the large and small leaves and the flower petals A, B and C, without seam allowances. Add a scant $^1/_4$ inch around each piece as you cut.

Black fabric
1. Using the template, cut five hexagon blocks and four half-hexagon blocks.

Yellow check fabric
1. Using the template, cut ten half-hexagon blocks.

Green fabric
1. Using templates, cut three edge triangles and two corner triangles.

2. Cut five full sets of leaves. Cut five straight grain strips, $^3/_4$ x $5^1/_4$ inches for the center stem and ten bias strips, $^3/_4$ x 6 inches for the curved stems.

3. For the half blocks, cut four small leaves and four large leaves. Cut four more bias strips, as above, for the curved stems.

Rose pink fabric
1. Cut six border strips, 5 x 36 inches.

2. Cut 30 squares, $1^1/_2$ x $1^1/_2$ inches and 15 squares, $1^7/_8$ x $1^7/_8$ inches, for the baskets. Cut the larger squares once diagonally to make 30 triangles.

3. Using Template B, cut 19 flowers.

Blue fabric
1. Cut six border strips, $6^1/_4$ x 36 inches.

2. Cut 55 squares, $1^1/_2$ x $1^1/_2$ inches.

Yellow fabric
1. Cut six border strips, $1^1/_2$ x 36 inches.

2. Cut two top border strips, $4^1/_2$ x 29 inches.

3. Using the templates, cut 19 A flower heads and 19 C center petals.

4. From the remainder, cut six strips, $1^1/_4$ inches wide across the full width of the fabric. Sew strips together to make a continuous length for separate binding.

PUTTING THE BLOCK TOGETHER

1. Crease the block down the center to help position the appliqué shapes.

2. Piece together the blue and pink squares in rows,

adding pink triangles at one end. Note that there are blue squares at the ends of the rows for the base of the basket.

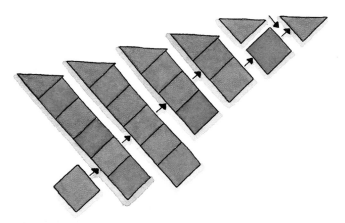

3. Press under and baste the seam allowance on the top and sides and position the basket on the block over the center line with the corners of the two lowest pink squares just coinciding with the seam allowance from the raw edge. Appliqué the basket to the background except for 2-3 inches at the center of the top edge where the stem will fit.

4. Baste the bottom edge of the block and the blue basket squares together within the block seam allowance, then trim the blue squares level with the block.

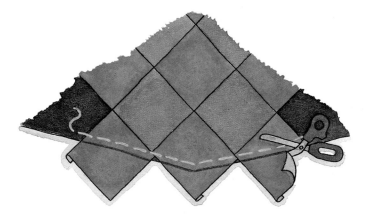

5. Fold the straight stem strip lengthwise into three and press. Place vertically on the center of the block with one end tucked under the edge of the basket. Baste then prepare the two curved stems in the same way. Position these on the block each with one end tucked under the center stem and baste.

6. Fingerpress the turnings on the leaves, then sew in position to the background, tucking the ends under the basted stem. When all the leaves are stitched, sew down the stems.

7. Fingerpress the turnings on a B flower, position over the end of the straight stem and sew, adding the small yellow flower head A in position.

8. Fingerpress the turnings on center petal C then appliqué in position on the B flower. Repeat to work the remaining two lilies.

9. Make five complete blocks, and four half blocks using a single curved stem and lily from the main design. Take care to position the flowers on the half blocks to face each other.

PUTTING THE QUILT TOGETHER

1. Lay out the blocks using the quilt as a guide. Assemble in horizontal rows, then join the rows together pivoting along the angled seams carefully. Inset two green edge triangles to the top of the quilt and one to the center of the bottom edge. Attach a corner triangle to each side of the bottom edge.

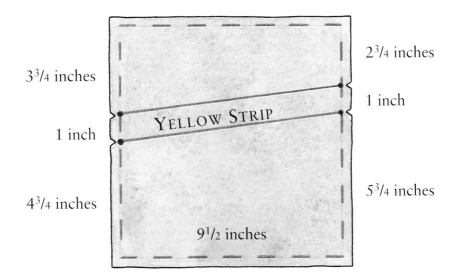

3³/4 inches

2³/4 inches

1 inch

YELLOW STRIP

1 inch

4³/4 inches

5³/4 inches

9¹/2 inches

2. Before sewing the borders, make a template to the measurements shown in the diagram. Use see-through plastic if possible; if using card, cut notches on the sides to mark the yellow strip position.

3. To make the borders, assemble the border strips into six sets, each with a pink, a narrow yellow and a blue strip. Press the seams on three sets towards the pink and on the others towards the blue. Place the template on the first strip so that the markings line up with the yellow strip; the square will be set at an angle on the strip. Mark and cut three border squares from this strip, then repeat on the other two strips from this group.

4. Take the second group (with the seams pressed the other way) and, making sure to turn over the template, cut three further border squares from each of the three strips.

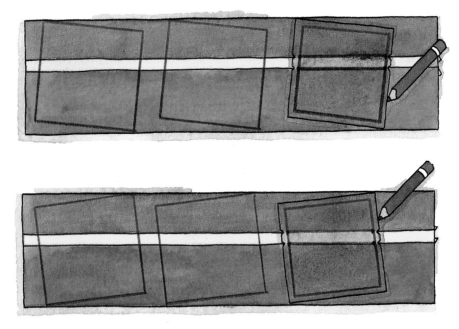

5. Each border needs three squares from each group arranged alternately to form the zigzag design. Lay the squares out, a set of six at a time, and sew together. The pressed seams should help with matching the zigzag yellow strip.

6. When complete, attach two borders to opposite sides of the quilt. Center, then attach the third border to the bottom edge.

7. Seam the $4^1/2$ inch wide yellow strips together then fold in half lengthwise and press. Stitch to the quilt top with a $1/4$ inch seam, keeping the border layers separate Press.

8. Divide the backing fabric into two equal lengths and machine stitch together with a $1/2$ inch seam allowance.

9. Trim away the selvedges and press.

10. Assemble the quilt layers, pin then baste thoroughly.

11. Quilt around the floral elements of the appliqué blocks and around the baskets, add lily sprigs in the setting blocks. Echo quilt $1/4$ inch away from the seams of the blocks and on each side of the yellow border zigzag.

12. Trim the batting and the backing even with the quilt top, except at the top edge where they should be trimmed level with the fold pressed in the yellow border strip. Fold this strip over to the back and sew in place. Baste the remaining raw edges together within the seam allowance, then add a narrow yellow binding to three sides to finish.

WATER LILIES

Here the stretched hexagon block is set horizontally and
interpreted in two ways, firstly with a watery print and secondly,
divided in two with a wavy line that is repeated in the border.
The water lily petals and leaves should be correctly positioned and
basted before beginning to slipstitch to the foundation.

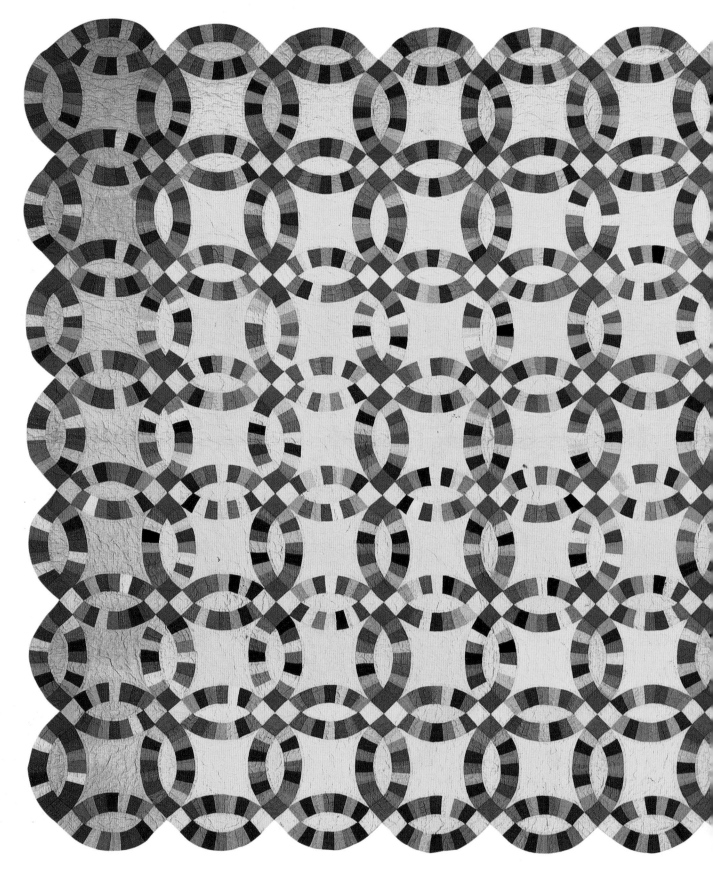

Art Deco Wedding Ring

DOUBLE WEDDING RING

To the non-quilting observer, the Double Wedding Ring is an intriguing design which appears not to have the usual block framework. It is also an impressive way to demonstrate piecing skills with all those tiny pieces and the curved seams, though as given here, recently devised techniques will ease the piecing of these small units.

In *Art Deco Wedding Ring*, the sprinkling of blue and yellow squares where the rings interlock adds a definitely modern appearance. *Pastel Rings* uses a black background with a graphic border to convey a strong Deco mood, while the red, white and blue color scheme of *Patriotic Wedding Rings* is one much used by quilters of all periods.

Skill level: Advanced
Quilt size: 72 x 82 inches
Finished block: 15 inches diameter
Number of blocks: 28 round blocks,
15 ellipse units

MATERIALS

Bright yellow 4 ¹/₈ yards
Blue ³/₈ yard
Scrap solid colors equivalent to 5 ¹/₄ yards
Backing 4 ¹/₄ yards
Batting 76 x 86 inches
Tracing paper for foundation paper piecing

CUTTING INSTRUCTIONS

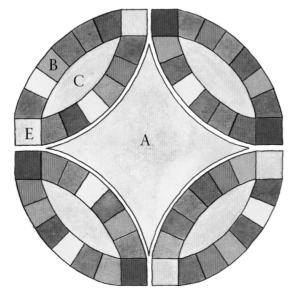

Make templates for pieces A and C to include a ¹/₄ inch seam allowance on all sides.

Bright yellow fabric
1. Using templates, cut 56 A pieces and 127 C pieces.

2. Cut 128 E squares, 2 x 2 inches.

Blue fabric
1. Cut 126 E squares, 2 x 2 inches.

Scrap solid colors
1. Using the foundation paper piecing technique makes it unnecessary to cut accurate small pieces for the pieced arcs. Scraps can be used and trimmed after stitching. If working with yardage, cut strips 2 ¹/₂ inches wide.

PUTTING THE BLOCK TOGETHER

1. Make eight tracings of the B unit from the template section onto tracing paper. The solid lines represent stitching lines. Mark ¹/₄ inch seam allowance.

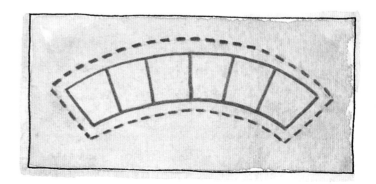

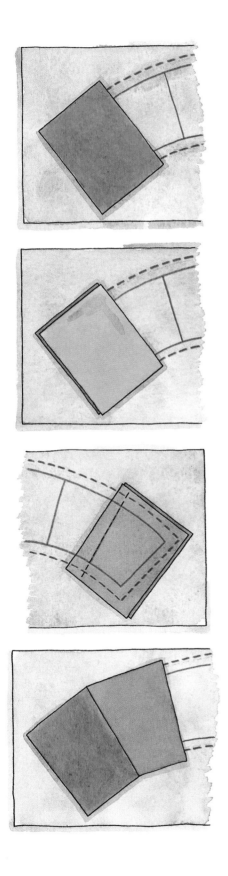

2. Piece the B units with your choice of assorted scrap fabrics. Place one foundation paper drawn-side down and lay the first piece of fabric, right side up, over one end of the shape, ensuring sufficient spare fabric for turnings on all sides.

Pin or hold with a dab of gluestick. Lay piece two over it, and pin with right sides together. Check that when the seam is sewn, this piece will open out to completely cover its marked position.

Turn the unit over and sew along the marked stitching line, starting and ending within the marked seam allowance.

3. Turn the work fabric side up, and trim to a $1/4$ inch seam allowance away from the stitching. Turn piece two over into position and fingerpress. Place piece three over piece two, right sides together, and repeat the process. Continue until all six patches are attached to this tracing.

4. Make eight B units in this way, then press and trim both fabric and foundations down to their marked seam allowances.

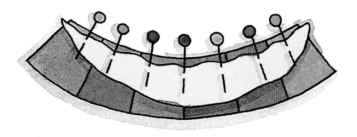

5. Place a C piece and a B unit right sides together and matching the notches carefully, pin securely at right angles to the sewing line.

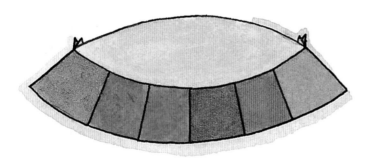

Stitch along the marked sewing line with the B unit on top. Repeat for a total of four units of joined C pieces and B units.

6. Attach a blue E square to each end of two B units and attach a yellow E square to each end of the remaining two B units.

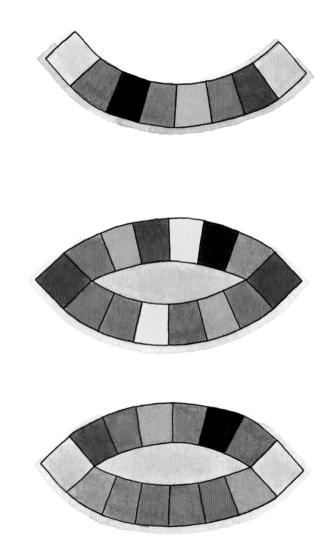

Attach one each of these to the units completed in step 5 to make four elliptical D units. Press.

7. Lay out one A piece then place the two D units with blue E squares top and bottom and the two D units with yellow E squares at the sides. Join the top and bottom D units to piece A, matching the curves and sewing carefully on the lines. Press. Repeat to attach the side D units.

8. Make 28 round blocks in this way. Note that this will use half of the A pieces cut.

9. Make 15 more D units, eight with two yellow E squares and seven with two blue E squares.

ASSEMBLING THE QUILT TOP

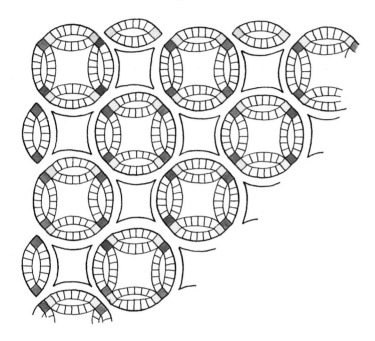

1. Lay the 28 round blocks, the 15 D units and the 28 A pieces out in position following the illustration.

2. Assemble into rows by joining the first round block to the A piece next to it, then joining the opposite side of the A piece to the next block and so on, as indicated. Note that alternate rows have D units at one side or the other. Press seams carefully.

3. Attach the D units at the top and bottom to complete the scalloped outline.

4. Complete the quilt top by sewing the rows to one another, carefully matching the meandering seams. To protect the edges of the quilt during completion, turn under the 1/4 inch seam allowance all around the outer edge and baste.

MARKING, QUILTING & FINISHING

1. Mark the quilting design in all A and C pieces.

2. Divide the backing fabric into two equal lengths and seam together with a 1/2 inch allowance. Trim away the selvedges and press the seam to one side.

3. Place the backing, right side down, on a flat surface. Center the batting and pieced top over the backing, then baste.

4. Quilt along the marked lines and add a line through the middle of each wedge in the pieced arcs.

5. After quilting, trim the batting level with the prepared edges of the quilt, following the curves closely. Trim the backing fabric to include 1/4 inch turnings. Fold these in over the batting so that they are level with the top edge. Sew the layers together along the edge to finish.

PASTEL RINGS

Skill level: Advanced
Quilt size: 69 x 84 inches
Finished block: 15 inches diameter
Number of blocks: 12

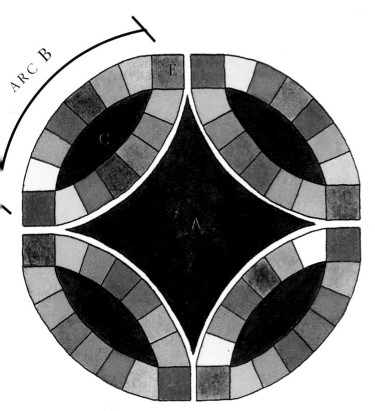

MATERIALS

Black 3 ¹/2 yards
White 2 yards
Dark green ³/8 yard
Violet blue ³/8 yard
Bright, dark and pastel scraps equivalent to
2 ¹/4 yards.
Backing 4 yards
Batting 73 x 88 inches
Tracing paper for foundation paper piecing

CUTTING INSTRUCTIONS

Make templates for pieces A, a half-A, quarter-A and
C to include a ¹/4 inch seam allowance on all sides.

Black fabric
1. Cut two G border strips, 74 x 7 inches;
two H border strips, 71 x 7 inches;
two C border strips, 66 x 2 ¹/2 inches;
two D border strips, 55 x 2 ¹/2 inches.

2. Using templates cut 18 A pieces, 10 half-A
pieces, four quarter-A pieces and 48 C pieces.

White fabric
1. Cut two E border strips, 70 x 2 ¹/2 inches;
two F border strips, 61 x 2 ¹/2 inches;
two A border strips, 62 x 2 ¹/2 inches;
and two B border strips, 51 x 2 ¹/2 inches.

2. Use the remaining fabric in the pieced arcs, if
required.

Dark green fabric
1. Cut 48 E squares, 2 x 2 inches.

Violet blue fabric
1. Cut 48 E squares, 2 x 2 inches.

Scrap solid colors
Using the foundation paper piecing technique
makes it unnecessary to cut accurate small pieces
for the pieced arcs. Small scraps of same-weight
fabric can be used and trimmed after stitching.
However, if working with yardage, cut strips
2 ¹/2 inches wide.

PUTTING THE QUILT TOGETHER

1. Following the instructions for foundation piecing given for *Art Deco Double Wedding Ring*, make up 12 round blocks, substituting dark green E pieces for the yellow ones. For this variation, attach one violet blue and one dark green E piece to each B unit in step 5 of the main quilt instructions.

2. Lay out the completed blocks according to the illustration, noting that the blocks are arranged with the E piece junctions top and bottom. Set the remaining A pieces in the spaces between the blocks and set the half-A and quarter-A pieces around the sides and at the corners to complete the quilt center.

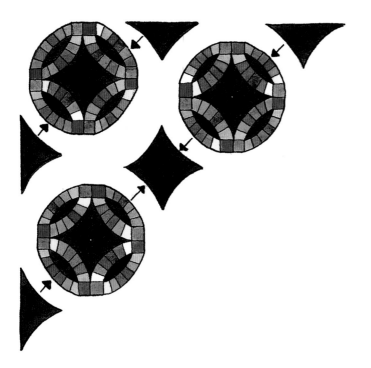

3. Assemble into diagonal rows as illustrated, matching seams carefully. Ensure that the half-A

pieces provide straight edges for the sides of the quilt. Press.

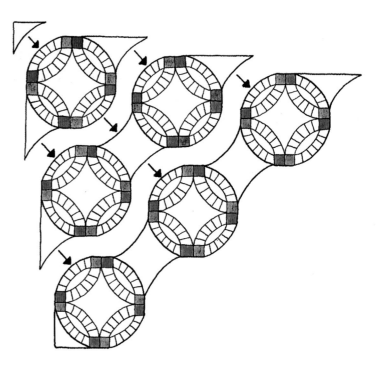

4. Join the diagonal rows to complete the center of the quilt and press.

5. Lay out the border strips in position around the center, in order, beginning with the A and B strips. Note that for each round of borders, the strips should be attached to the top and bottom before those at the side. Attach all strips in the correct sequence ensuring that the corners remain square. Press.

6. Lay the completed top on a firm surface and mark the quilting design as for *Art Deco Double Wedding Ring*. The outer border is quilted with a grid of angled parallel lines that can be marked with masking tape.

7. Divide the backing fabric into two equal lengths. Sew a $^1/_2$ inch seam down one long side, then cut away the selvedges. Press the seam to one side.

8. Place the backing right side down on a flat surface. Center the batting then the quilt top over the backing, right side up. Baste the layers together thoroughly, starting from the center and working out diagonally, vertically and horizontally to the sides.

9. Work the quilting design in the A pieces and quilt in-the-ditch along the inner borders. Work the quilting in the outer border when the edges are finished.

10. The outer border of the quilt top has been cut to include $^3/_4$ inch to turn over to the back of the quilt for binding. Trim the batting and backing $^3/_4$ inch smaller than the quilt top on each side. Turn $^3/_4$ inch to the back, fold in $^1/_4$ inch along the raw edges and slipstitch into place. Complete quilting the outer border.

PATRIOTIC WEDDING RING

Skill level: Advanced
Quilt size: 47 x 47 inches
Finished block: 15 inches diameter
Number of blocks: 8

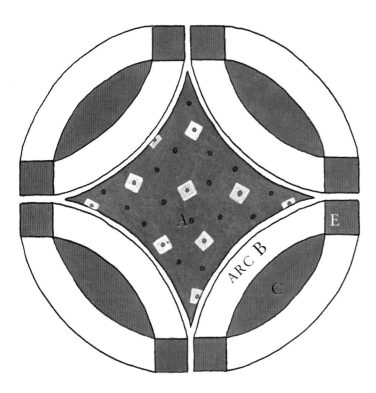

MATERIALS

Blue 1 ¼ yards
White 1 ½ yards
Red 1 yard
Backing 2 ¾ yards
Batting 50 x 50 inches

CUTTING INSTRUCTIONS

Make templates for pieces A, B and C to include a ¼ inch seam allowance on all sides. Note that in this variation the curved "ring" unit is a single fabric piece.

Blue fabric
1. Using the template, cut 16 A pieces.

White fabric
1. Using the template, cut 80 B pieces.

Red fabric
1. Using the template, cut 40 C pieces.

2. Cut 80 E squares, 2 x 2 inches.

PUTTING THE QUILT TOGETHER

1. Sew a red C piece to the inside curve of 40 white B pieces. Press.

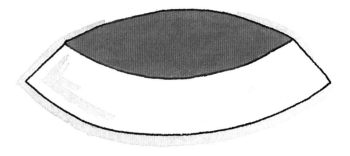

2. Attach a red E square to each end of the remaining 40 white B pieces. Press.

Then sew one of these units to each of the units assembled in step 1 above. This gives 40 elliptical D units.

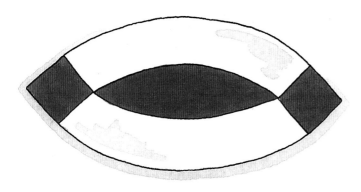

3. To assemble a round block, lay out a blue A piece with a D unit on each side. Join the top and bottom D units to an A piece and press, then repeat to add the side D units.

4. Make a total of eight round blocks. Eight D units will remain.

5. Lay out the round blocks as in the illustration adding the remaining A pieces and D units to complete the design.

6. Join the blocks in columns, by joining the first round block to the A piece below, then attaching the next block to the opposite side of piece A. Note that columns alternately end and start with set D units. Assemble four columns then attach the side D units to the first and last column. Join the columns together carefully matching the meandering seams.

7. Turn under and baste $1/4$ inch all round the outside edge. Divide the backing fabric into two equal lengths and join together with a $1/2$ inch seam allowance. Trim away the selvedges and press the seam to one side.

8. Assemble the quilt layers and baste thoroughly.

9. Quilt in-the ditch around the rings and fill the A pieces with a square grid on point. Quilt a square on point over each group of four red E squares.

10. Trim the batting even with the basted edge of the top. Trim the backing to leave a border of $1/4$ inch on all sides. Fold this over the batting and pin or baste in place.

11. To finish, slipstitch the folded edge of the backing to the basted edge of the top following the contoured scalloped edge.

BLUE AND WHITE RINGS

Inspiration for quilt designs can come in unusual places and be realized by a combination of techniques. A printed narrow stripe, as used in the elliptical patches, is shown developed here into a quilting design of bull's eyes. After quilting concentric circles in colored thread, the running stitches are whipped with the same thread to embolden the design.

Art Deco Snail Trails

SNAIL TRAILS

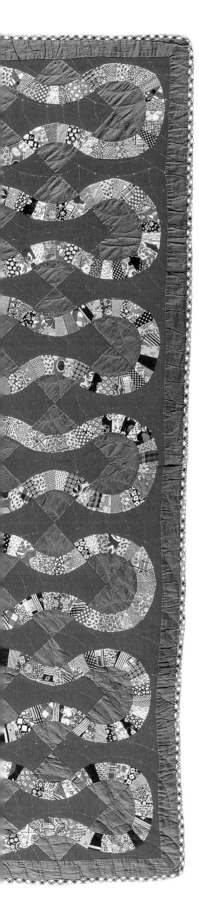

The Snail Trails design is formed by the careful placement of two opposing fans set within a block. When placed together, the fan-like arcs turn into a wonderfully flowing line which, as the quilts given here demonstrate, can construct a variety of designs.

Art Deco Snail Trails is a formal version, each fan pieced in a variety of colorful prints. The curved line connects back up with itself to form extended loops. *Happy Trails* shows just what exciting possibilities exist for the wavy line design element. Its crazy-pieced background is reminiscent of the work of artists of the period, such as the Delaunays. The quilter embarking on this project could assemble the blocks worked into an entirely unique version of the design, as is also possible with *Jazz*. Here, realized in a classic period color scheme, what is basically a single design line is echoed and reinforced over the whole quilt.

Skill level: Intermediate
Quilt size: 67 $\frac{3}{8}$ x 85 $\frac{3}{4}$ inches
Finished block: 6 $\frac{1}{2}$ x 6 $\frac{1}{2}$ inches
Number of blocks: 104 blocks, 32 half blocks

MATERIALS

Green 2 $\frac{1}{4}$ yards
Red 4 $\frac{1}{2}$ yards
Scrap prints equivalent to 4 $\frac{1}{2}$ yards
Backing 4 yards
Batting 71 x 89 $\frac{3}{4}$ inches
Green plaid for binding $\frac{3}{8}$ yard
Tracing paper for foundation paper piecing

CUTTING INSTRUCTIONS

Make templates for A pieces, half-A pieces and corner C pieces. Add $\frac{1}{4}$ inch seam allowances when cutting out. No template is required for the small pieces in the pieced arc B because you will be using the foundation paper machine-piecing technique.

Green fabric

1. Cut four strips, 2 inches wide, across the full width of the fabric. Label for the long borders and set aside. For the short borders, cut two strips, 2 x 70 inches from the fabric length. Trim away selvedges before cutting the strips.

2. From the remaining fabric, cut 240 corner C pieces.

Red fabric

1. Using templates, cut 104 A pieces and 32 half-A pieces. When cutting the half-A pieces, place the long diagonal on the straight grain of the fabric, if possible.

Scrap Prints

1. Using the foundation paper piecing technique makes it unnecessary to cut accurate small pieces for the pieced arcs. Scraps can be used and trimmed after stitching. When working from yardage, cut strips 2 $\frac{1}{2}$ inches wide.

PUTTING THE BLOCK TOGETHER

1. To make one block, first make two tracings of arc B from the template section onto tracing paper. The solid line is the stitching line. Add $\frac{1}{4}$ inch for seam allowances.

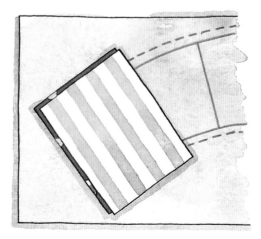

2. Place one foundation paper drawn-side down and lay the first piece of fabric right side up over one of the end shapes. Make sure to allow for the

seam allowances. Pin or hold with a dab of gluestick. Lay the second print fabric over the first, and pin with right sides together. Check that once the seam is sewn, the second piece will open out to cover its correct position with sufficient fabric.

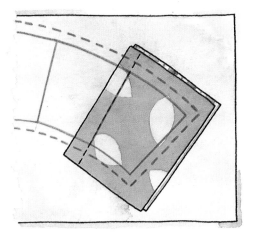

3. Turn the unit over and sew along the drawn stitching line. Turn the work, fabric side up, and trim to leave a $^1/_4$ inch seam allowance.

Open out the second piece and fingerpress. Place piece three over piece two, right sides together, and repeat the process. Continue until all six pieces are stitched to the tracing. Repeat to work a second

arc. Press with a dry iron but do not remove the papers.

4. To insert the corner C pieces, find the center of the curved edge by folding lightly in half then match this to the midpoint of the inside curve of

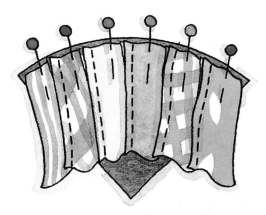

pieced arc B and pin. Match and pin the outer ends of the seam, then pin at right angles across the seam, clipping the inside curve as necessary. Sew the seam carefully, with the tracing on top to follow the drawn line. Repeat to insert the second corner C piece into the remaining pieced arc B.

5. Insert these units into piece A in the same way. Press and remove the papers.

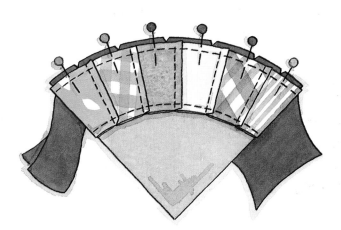

6. Make 104 blocks and 32 triangular half blocks, using the same process.

ASSEMBLING THE QUILT TOP

1. Starting with a row of eight complete blocks set on point, lay out the quilt alternating between rows of eight and nine blocks. Use triangular half-blocks at the corners and to fill in the spaces at the sides.

2. Sew the blocks together in diagonal rows, making sure that the pieced B arcs on adjacent blocks meet up accurately to allow the "trail" to flow.

3. Join the diagonal rows together, matching the pieced B arcs and the block intersections and easing the seams when necessary.

4. Sew the two 2 x 70 inch border strips to the short sides of the quilt using a ¹/₄ inch seam allowance. Press the seams to one side. Join the full width strips in pairs with ¹/₂ inch seams and press open. Then attach to the long sides of the quilt.

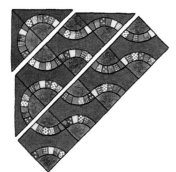

MARKING, QUILTING & FINISHING

1. With the quilt top on a firm surface, mark the quilting design. The quilt illustrated was worked with an all over pattern called *Baptist Fan*, a series of concentric arcs which can be marked using the simple strip template supplied. Hold an end of the template at the corner of a block, insert the point of a pencil in a hole. Swing the pencil to mark an even arc. Repeat with each hole.

2. Divide the backing fabric into two equal lengths. With right sides together, sew a ¹/₂ inch allowance. Trim away the selvedges and press the seam to one side.

3. Lay the backing fabric on a flat surface, right side down. Center the batting and quilt top over it. Pin, then baste thoroughly.

4. Quilt along the marked lines.

5. Trim the edges of the backing and batting even with the top. Use the green plaid fabric to make a continuous bias strip, following the directions in the Techniques section. Baste around the edge of the quilt inside the seam allowance. Pin binding to the front of the quilt, matching raw edges. Sew through all layers with a ¹/₄ inch seam allowance. Turn the folded edge of the binding to the back of the quilt, enclosing the batting and raw edges, and slipstitch in place.

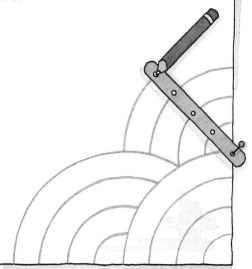

JAZZ

Skill level: Beginner/Intermediate
Finished block: 6 $^1/_2$ x 6 $^1/_2$ inches
Finished quilt: 64 $^1/_2$ x 51 $^1/_2$ inches
Number of blocks: 63

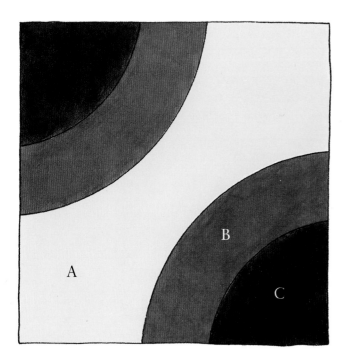

MATERIALS

Yellow 2 yards
Black 1 yard
Black print ³/4 yard
Red 1 ¹/2 yards
Backing 3 yards
Batting 68 x 55 ¹/2 inches

CUTTING INSTRUCTIONS

Make templates for piece A, arc B and corner C, including ¹/4 inch seam allowance for machine piecing.

Yellow fabric
1. Using Template A, cut 63 pieces.

Black solid & black print
1. Cut two side border strips, each 3¹/2 x 61 inches and one border strip for the bottom, 3¹/2 x 60 inches.

2. Using the template, cut 126 corner C pieces.

3. From the remaining fabric cut 7 yards of binding strips or make a continuous bias binding strip as directed in the Techniques section.

Red fabric
1. Using the template, cut 126 B arcs.

PUTTING THE QUILT TOGETHER

1. Following the instructions for *Art Deco Snail Trails*, but using the templates, cut A, B and C pieces. Make 63 blocks.

2. On a flat surface lay out the blocks using the quilt illustration as a guide. If creating a different layout, make a sketch to follow for the correct orientation of each block. Join the blocks into rows, checking direction and matching the B arcs accurately. Join the rows to complete the top.

3. Add the 61 inch border strips to the sides of the quilt and trim. Add the remaining border strip to the bottom edge of the quilt.

4. With the quilt on a firm surface, mark the quilting design using the *Baptist Fan* pattern for *Art Deco Snail Trails*.

5. Divide the backing fabric into two equal halves and seam together.

6. Place the backing right side down on a flat surface. Center the batting then the quilt top over the backing, right side up. Baste the layers together thoroughly, starting from the center and working out diagonally, vertically and horizontally to the sides.

7. Quilt along the marked lines.

8. Using the black strips, follow the Separate binding method as described in the Techniques section to finish the quilt.

HAPPY TRAILS

Skill level: Beginner/Intermediate
Quilt size: 45 $\frac{1}{2}$ x 58 $\frac{1}{2}$ inches
Finished block: 6 $\frac{1}{2}$ x 6 $\frac{1}{2}$ inches
Number of blocks: 63

MATERIALS

Electric blue 1 $\frac{1}{2}$ yards
Solid color scraps equivalent to $\frac{3}{4}$ yard
Scrap prints and solids equivalent to 2 yards
Backing / binding 2 $\frac{5}{8}$ yards / metres
Batting 62 $\frac{1}{2}$ x 49 $\frac{1}{2}$ inches
Tracing paper for foundation paper piecing

CUTTING INSTRUCTIONS

Make templates for arc B and corner C pieces,

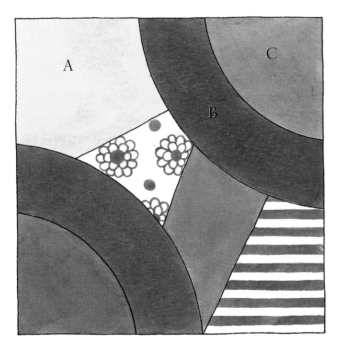

including a $\frac{1}{4}$ inch seam allowance for machine piecing.

Electric blue fabric

1. Using template, cut 126 B arcs.

Solid color scraps

1. Cut a total of 126 corner C pieces from a mixture of fabrics.

Scrap prints and solids

1. Shape A is crazy-pieced so pre-cutting is not necessary.

PUTTING THE BLOCK TOGETHER

1. Trace Template A onto tracing paper. Cut out to include $\frac{1}{4}$ inch seam allowances. This forms the foundation on which random scraps will be sewn.

2. Place scraps over the foundation until you are pleased with the arrangement. Lay the first scrap on the paper, right side up. Place another scrap over it, right side down, matching one raw edge. Sew parallel to this edge using a short stitch length, taking a $\frac{1}{4}$ inch seam. Open out the pieces and press lightly with a dry iron. Continue adding scraps to cover shape A. Use a gluestick to hold end pieces to the paper or baste to hold them in place.

3. Insert corner C pieces into the B arcs following the instructions for *Art Deco Snail Trails*. Attach these assembled units to the crazy-pieced A shapes as previously described. Press carefully, then remove the foundation tracing paper.

4. Make 63 blocks in this way.

PUTTING THE QUILT TOGETHER

1. Lay out the blocks on a flat surface and build the blue snail trail design using the quilt as a guide.

2. Sew the blocks together in rows, matching the blue arcs carefully at the seams. Join the rows to complete the top.

3. Divide the backing fabric into two equal lengths. Place right sides together and sew a $^1/_2$ inch seam along one long edge. Trim away the selvedges and press.

4. Assemble the quilt layers and baste together, starting in the center of the quilt and working out diagonally, horizontally and vertically.

5. Echo quilt $^1/_4$ in lines along side the blue trails and in concentric circles to fill the areas where the trail makes almost a full circle. Add extra quilting lines, if required, to remaining areas.

6. After quilting, use the Self-binding method to finish the raw edges as described in the Techniques section.

SNAKE EYES

Extra design lines are pieced in this block to bring the opposing
curves together in the middle of the block and to provide the little
dark corners. When the blocks are set this way, they take on a
completely different appearance, giving this quilt
its distinctive name.

Art Deco Diamond Stars

DIAMONDS

The diamond is an enduringly popular design. Its simple tessellating shape when colored in different ways can create a multitude of designs. Bright, colored stars set against a rich, black ground give *Diamond Stars* its modern appearance. The stepped border is an unusual touch but consistent with the design preferences of the period.

In *Tumbling Blocks*, the careful placement of light, medium and dark diamonds creates a three-dimensional "concertina" effect.

Blazing Star is a favorite with many quiltmakers. Its ability to create a pulsating image must also have appealed to a generation exploring the power and potential of color.

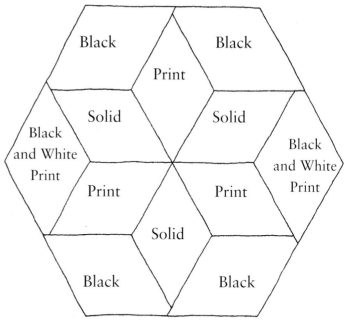

Skill level: Advanced
Finished block: 6 x 6 inches
Finished quilt: 80 x 80 inches
Number of blocks: 224

MATERIALS

Black 4 yards
Black and white print 2 yards
Co-ordinating solid and print fabrics 224 strips
    of each, at least $2^{1}/_{2}$ x $10^{1}/_{2}$ inches
Backing $4^{3}/_{4}$ yards
Batting 84 x 84 inches
Bias binding $9^{1}/_{4}$ yards

Each star is made up of two co-ordinated fabrics; a solid and print alternating between points. Black and white print diamonds are set into the angles to form hexagons.

CUTTING INSTRUCTIONS

To make a reusable template, first trace around the shape, cut out carefully and glue it to heavy card. Alternatively, trace directly onto template plastic. Place the template on the wrong side of the fabric and mark out the diamonds with a well-sharpened hard pencil. The pencil line is your sewing line. Add $^{1}/_{4}$ inch seam allowance all around each diamond as you cut.

To quick-cut these diamonds, first fold the fabric in half matching selvedges and press. Use a ruler to mark out strips, $2^{1}/_{4}$ inches wide across the full width of the fabric. Cut the fabric into strips, then place the template on the fabric and trace.

Black and white print fabric
1. Cut 448 diamonds. You will need two for each block.

Black fabric
1. Cut 896 diamonds. You will need four for each block.

Solid and print scraps
1. For each of the 224 blocks, cut three solid and three print diamonds. Pin each set of six diamonds together and set aside.

PUTTING THE BLOCK TOGETHER

Hand-piecing is recommended for this quilt because its many angles require insetting to achieve the mosaic-like effect.

1. Pin and sew a solid and print diamond right sides together, raw edges matching. Start and finish your seam exactly on the pencil  line. Do not stitch into the seam allowance. fingerpress the seam towards the darker side.

2. Sew another solid diamond to the raw edge of the print diamond to make half the star. The two seams will meet at the center.

3. Make another three-patch unit in the same way, but reverse the color sequence to two print diamonds with the solid in the middle position.

4. Sew the two halves together; at the center point, pass the needle through the layers of fabric and continue sewing the seam across the center seam. On the wrong side, press all seams in the same direction and spiral the center seam allowances so they lie flat.

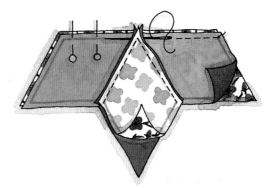

5. Referring to the block diagram, position a black and white diamond at opposite sides of the star. With right sides together and raw edges matching, stitch along one side of the diamond on the pencil line. Pivot the diamond to align it with the edge of the next diamond, pass the needle through the intersection, and continue the seam.

6. Inset the other black and white diamond in position by following the same stitching sequence.

7. Inset four solid black diamonds in the remaining gaps to form a hexagon.

8. Spiral seams at each intersection to reduce bulk and press.

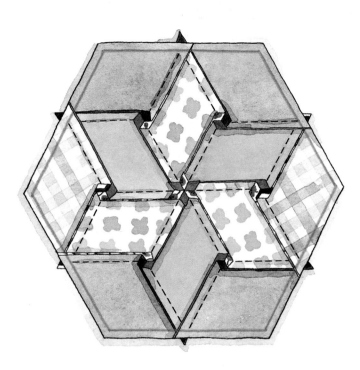

9. Make 223 more blocks in the same way.

PUTTING THE QUILT TOGETHER

1. Lay out the hexagonal blocks into 16 rows of 14 each. Be sure to position all hexagons in the same orientation, with the two solid-colored diamonds in the top half of the block.

2. Sew the blocks into rows, then sew the rows together by insetting hexagons into the gaps. "Offset" the rows to create the scalloped contour edge at the top and bottom.

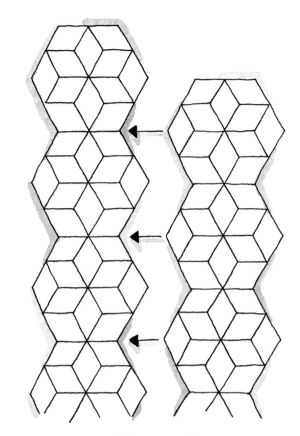

3. Cut the length of backing fabric into two equal pieces. With right sides facing and selvedges matching, sew a 1/2 inch seam down one edge. Cut off selvedges, then press seam to one side.

4. Place the backing right side down on a large flat surface. Center the batting and quilt top, right side up, onto the backing, and baste together.

5. Quilt around each of the diamonds, 3/8 inch from the seams.

6. When quilting is complete, trim the batting and backing even with the quilt top.

7. Finish the raw edges with Continuous bias binding.

BLAZING STAR

Skill level: Advanced.
Quilt size: 68 x 75 inches
Central star: 54 x 54 inches

MATERIALS

$^3/_4$ yard each of pink, red, green and white for Star
    panel, inner border and binding
Batting 71 x 78 inches
$3^1/_4$ yards navy blue for background, and
    outer border
Backing 4 yards

A large eight-pointed star forms the central motif
of this quilt. Each segment of the star is made up of
eight rows of eight diamonds in four colors. The
inner border is pieced using diamonds in the same
color and scale as the star. Machine-piecing is
recommended, but the instructions can be adapted
if traditional hand-sewing techniques are preferred.

CUTTING INSTRUCTIONS

Navy blue fabric
1. Cut two border strips, $8^1/_2$ x 58 $^1/_8$ inches and
two strips, $5^1/_2$ x 74 $^1/_8$ inches across the lengthwise
grain.

2. For the background triangles, cut one square,
23 $^7/_8$ x 23 $^7/_8$ inches and divide into four
diagonally. This ensures that the straight grain will
run parallel with the sides of the quilt.

3. For the corner squares, cut four squares, $16^1/_2$ x
$16^1/_2$ inches.

Pink, Red, Green and White fabric
1. From each color, cut ten strips, 2 inches / 5.1 cm
wide across the full width of the fabric. These
strips will be used to quick-piece the star segments
and inner border.

2. For the binding, cut two full width strips,
2 inches wide from each of the pink and green
fabrics.

PUTTING THE STAR TOGETHER

1. Sew strips together in the following
combinations:
Set 1: pink-red-green-white-pink-red-green-white
Set 2: red-green-white-pink-red-green-white-pink
Set 3: green-white-pink-red-green-white-pink-red
Set 4: white-pink-red-green-white-pink-red-green

Take great care to use an exact $^1/_4$ inch seam
allowance. Press.

2. For the pieced inner border, sew another set in a
combination of your choice.

3. Align the 45° angle on your quilter's ruler with
one of the inside seams. Then use your rotary
cutter to cut 16 diagonal strips, a scant 2 inches
wide from each strip set. This step requires great
precision. After cutting two or three strips, you
may need to re-adjust the cut edge by trimming to
a true 45° angle.

4. Sew pieced strips together in sequence to make eight star points.

5. Sew star points together into four pairs, ending the seam $^1/_4$ inch from the edge. This will leave your seam allowance free to inset the blue background pieces.

6. Sew two quarters together to make half of the star. To complete the star, join the two halves. Remember to stop the seam $^1/_4$ inch from the raw edge.

7. To inset the corner squares and side triangles, first pin the shapes to the pieced star point with raw edges matching, and right sides facing. Starting from the inside corner, stitch towards the point of the star segment. Then pivot the shape to align it with the raw edge of the adjacent side. Continue stitching the seam to the end.

8. For the inner border, join pieced strips together, end to end, to make four long strips.

9. Sew the pieced border strips to the sides of the quilt. Press, then sew the remaining two pieced borders to the top and bottom.

10. Sew the broad blue borders to the quilt following the same sequence. Press.

11. Mark the quilting pattern with a sharp white or gray pencil, cross-hatching in a grid on the plain areas and large cable design on the borders. The diamonds will be outline quilted so they do not require marking.

12. Assemble the three layers, baste and quilt. Finish the raw edges with Separate binding as described in the Techniques section.

TUMBLING BLOCKS

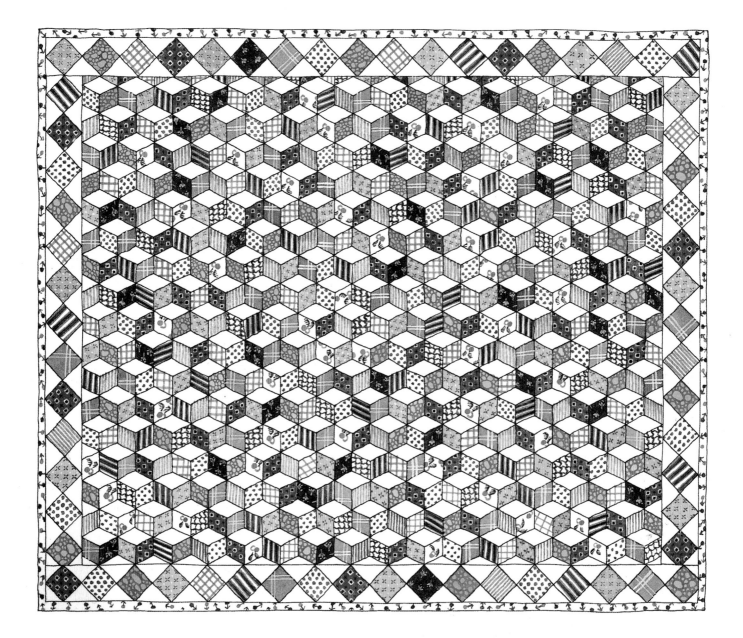

Skill level: Intermediate
Quilt size: 53 $\frac{1}{2}$ x 56 inches
Number of Star blocks: 72

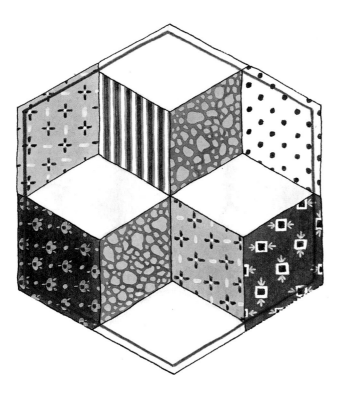

MATERIALS

1/2 yard each of four different dark, medium and
   light fabrics for contrast diamonds and border
   squares
2 1/4 yards light fabric for the background
Batting one piece 58 x 60 inches
Backing / binding 3 1/4 yards

CUTTING INSTRUCTIONS

Assorted contrast fabrics
1. Cut 544 diamonds using the diamond template.
You will need about 45 diamonds from each of the
12 different fabrics. Add 1/4 inch seam allowance
around each shape as you cut.

2. Cut 32 using the quarter diamonds to complete
the pattern at the edge of the quilt.

3. Cut 62 squares, 3 x 3 inches for the border.

Light background fabric
1. Cut 297 diamonds for the central design.

2. Cut 58 squares, 3 3/8 x 3 3/8 inches in half
diagonally for the pieced diamond border.

PUTTING THE QUILT TOGETHER

1. Sort contrast diamonds into dark, medium and
light values. Follow the same sequence to hand-
piece the diamonds as for *Art Deco Diamond
Stars*. For each star, sew two halves together, each
consisting of three diamonds. The light diamonds
must be in the middle position of each half.

2. With the center seam of the star block running
vertically, and the light diamonds side by side, inset
two light diamonds into the top and bottom gaps.
Use four contrasting diamonds to fill in the
remaining gaps.

3. Join the resulting hexagons together, filling in
the edges by insetting the appropriate colored
diamond. Trim excess diamonds, leaving 1/4 inch
seam allowance to straighten the raw edges at the
top, bottom and sides.

4. Construct border strips by sewing the light
background triangles to opposite sides of the
contrast squares to make short diagonal strips.

5. Sew the diagonal strips together into two lengths
of 18 squares, for the top and bottom, and two
lengths of 13 squares, for the sides.

6. Pin, then sew the longer border strips to the top and bottom, cutting away the excess as before.

7. Prepare the backing fabric by trimming off selvedges and seaming two widths together. Press seam allowances to one side.

8. Press and tidy the quilt top. Then assemble the three quilt layers carefully. Place the backing right side down on a flat surface. Center the batting then the quilt top over the backing, right side up. Baste the layers together thoroughly, starting from the center and working out diagonally, vertically and horizontally to the sides.

9. Quilt in parallel lines, $1\frac{1}{2}$ inches apart.

10. Finally, bring the backing around to the front to finish the raw edges using the Self-binding method as described in the Techniques section.

FRACTURED DIAMONDS

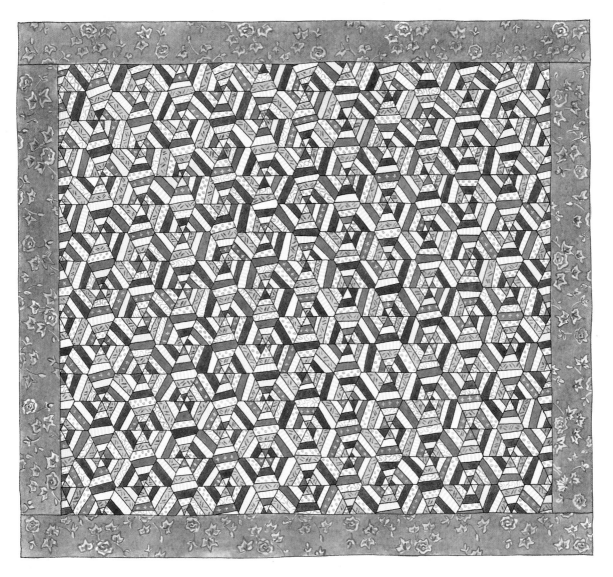

This final variation performs optical tricks, sometimes making cut-glass diamonds and sometimes three-dimensional hexagonal boxes. A simple method of string-piecing diamonds over a paper foundation would be the ideal way to construct this quilt. Many diamonds have strips of alternating blues and yellows, but in some cases, this rhythm is altered which helps to create the shifting, broken effect of the overall design.

Art Deco Fans

FANS

The fan motif is a signature for the Art Deco period, and for many people without specialized design education, it is the most readily identifiable symbol of the period. The fan block, already a popular design, was consequently assured a continuing place in the quilters' repertoire. The basic fan block has been reinterpreted in our first version — surely by someone who had seen glass shades for wall-lights — and the yellow side triangles have a bright, new modern look. The other designs show some of the possibilities which emerge when setting the fan blocks together in different ways.

The use of crazy piecing, which was popular at the end of the nineteenth century, is a surprising variation. It might be a continuing practical use of the scrapbag or just possibly, twentieth-century quilters saw the fractured planes of color in contemporary paintings and became inspired.

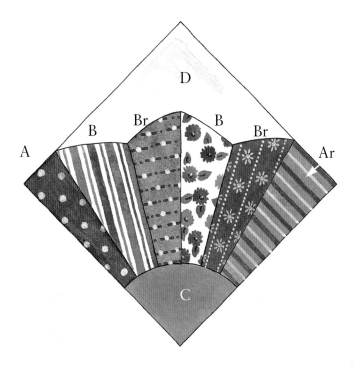

Skill Level: Intermediate
Finished block: $7^1/2$ x $7^1/2$ inches
Quilt size: $86^1/4$ x $75^1/2$ inches
Number of blocks: 98

MATERIALS

Yellow $1^1/8$ yards
White for background $2^1/4$ yards
Green 1 yard
14 scrap prints each $1/2$ yard
Backing $4^1/2$ yards
Batting 89 x 78 inches

CUTTING INSTRUCTIONS

Make templates for pieces A, B and C, including a $1/4$ inch seam allowance for machine- piecing. For hand-piecing, cut and trace templates on the solid line, then add seam allowances as you cut. Note that templates A and B are reversed to cut pieces Ar and Br.

Yellow fabric

1. Cut seven squares, $12^1/4$ x $12^1/4$ inches. Cut across both diagonals to make 28 side triangles; there will be two triangles extra.

2. Cut two squares, $6^1/4$ x $6^1/4$ inches diagonally in half to make four corner triangles.

White fabric

1. Cut 49 squares, 8 x 8 inches in half diagonally to make 98 D triangles for the background.

Green fabric

1. Using the template, cut 98 C quarter-circles.

Scrap prints

1. Using the templates, cut 98 A pieces, 98 Ar pieces, 196 B pieces and 196 Br pieces.

PUTTING THE BLOCK TOGETHER

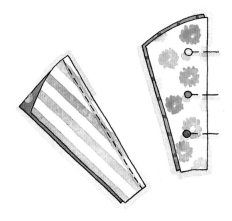

1. To make the fan unit, first sew one A piece to one B piece, then one Br piece to one B piece.

2. Sew one Br piece to one Ar piece.

Then, join the three pairs together in the correct sequence.

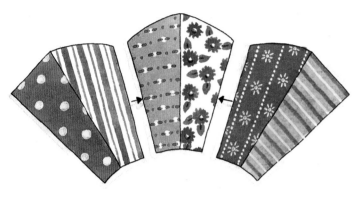

3. Turn under the curved edge of the quarter-circle C by pressing the seam allowance over a template.

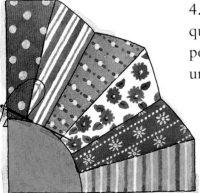

4. Set the prepared quarter circle C, in position over the fan unit and appliqué.

5. Place the fan unit over the white background D triangle so that the A and Ar pieces are aligned to the edges of the triangle and appliqué in position.

6. Press then trim away the excess background fabric from behind the fan, leaving ¼ inch seam allowance only.

7. Make a total of 98 blocks.

ASSEMBLING THE QUILT TOP

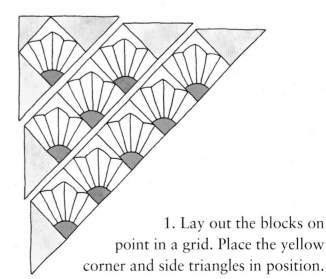

1. Lay out the blocks on point in a grid. Place the yellow corner and side triangles in position.

2. Pin, then sew blocks together in diagonal rows. Press seam allowances of adjacent rows in alternate directions.

3. Sew the diagonal rows first in pairs and continue until the top is complete. Press.

MARKING, QUILTING & FINISHING

1. Press the quilt top and trim away any loose threads which may show through to the front.

2. Choose a quilting design for the side triangles and the block backgrounds, and mark the quilt top with a sharp pencil.

3. Divide the backing fabric into two equal lengths. With right sides facing and selvedges matching, join lengths together using a $1/2$ inch seam. Trim away the selvedges and press the seam to one side.

4. Place the backing right side down on a flat surface. Center the batting then the quilt top over the backing, right side up. Baste the layers together thoroughly.

5. Quilt the marked designs and echo quilt or quilt in-the-ditch around the fans. Do not complete the quilting at the edges but leave about 2-3 inches until after the edges are finished.

6. Trim the side triangles leaving a $1/4$ inch seam allowance.

7. Finish the quilt using the Self-binding method by bringing the backing fabric to the front of the quilt, as described in the Techniques section.

PASTEL CRIB QUILT

Skill Level: Beginner
Quilt size: 43 $\frac{1}{2}$ x 43 $\frac{1}{2}$ inches
Finished block: 7 $\frac{1}{2}$ x 7 $\frac{1}{2}$ inches
Number of blocks: 16

MATERIALS

Cream for background $^{1}/_{2}$ yard
Cream for fan corners $^{1}/_{4}$ yard
Scrap prints equivalent to 1 $^{1}/_{4}$ yards
Pink $^{7}/_{8}$ yard
Green $^{1}/_{2}$ yard
Backing 1 $^{1}/_{4}$ yards
Batting 45 x 45 inches
Binding 5 $^{1}/_{2}$ yards

CUTTING INSTRUCTIONS

Make templates for pieces A, B and C following the instructions and block diagram for the *Art Deco Fans*.

Cream fabric

1. Cut eight squares, 8 x 8 inches in half diagonally, for the D background triangles.

2. If using the cream for the inner corners of the fan, cut 16 quarter circles with Template C. Alternatively, cut these from a contrasting fabric.

Scrap prints

1. Using templates, cut 16 each of A and Ar pieces and 32 each of B and Br pieces.

Pink fabric

1. Cut eight strips, 2 x 15 $^{1}/_{2}$ inches for the inner border.

2. Cut 16 strips, 2 x 18 $^{1}/_{2}$ inches for inner and outer borders. Note that these measurements are precise and do not include any excess.

3. Cut 13 squares, 2 x 2 inches for the corner squares.

Green fabric

1. Cut 12 strips, 2 x 18 $^{1}/_{2}$ inches for the middle border.

2. Cut 12 squares, 2 x 2 inches for the corner squares.

Binding

1. Cut 5 strips, 1 $^{1}/_{4}$ inches wide and join together to make a continuous length of 5 $^{1}/_{2}$ yards.

PUTTING THE BLOCKS TOGETHER

1. Following instructions for *Art Deco Fans*, make 16 fan blocks.

2. Arrange the blocks in groups of four with the C quarter circles at the four corners. Sew the blocks together first in pairs, side by side. Press the seams, then join pairs together. Make four large blocks, each consisting of four blocks.

PUTTING THE QUILT TOGETHER

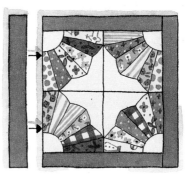

1. Lay out the four large blocks together with the sashing strips, border strips and corner squares.

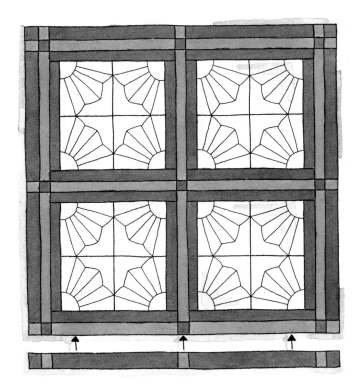

2. Following the sequence in the diagrams, sew the sashing strips and corner squares to the four large blocks. Press before sewing on borders.

3. Place the backing right side down on a flat surface. Center the batting then the quilt top over the backing, right side up. Baste the layers together thoroughly, starting from the center and working out diagonally, vertically and horizontally to the sides.

4. Echo quilt the corner quarter circles and quilt $1/4$ inch from the edge of each fan segment. Fill the remaining block area with a simple grid, and quilt in-the-ditch around the sashing and borders.

5. Finish the raw edges of the quilt using the Separate binding method as described in the Techniques section.

CRAZY FANS

Skill Level: Beginner
Quilt size: 60 x 68 inches
Finished block: 7 1/2 x 7 1/2 inches
Number of blocks: 36

MATERIALS

Assorted dark colors for fan corners 3/8 yard
Assorted bright colors equivalent to 3 3/4 yards
Background colors 1 yard
Assorted plaids and solid colors equivalent to
 2 yards for borders
Backing 4 yards
Batting 62 x 70 inches
Binding 7 1/2 yards
Embroidery thread or crochet cotton for tying

CUTTING INSTRUCTIONS

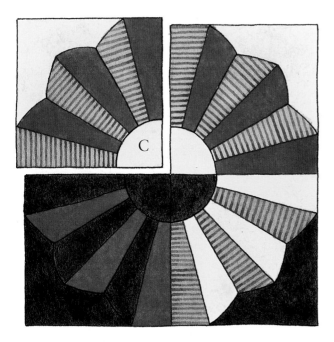

Make templates for pieces A, B and C following
the instructions and block diagram for the *Art
Deco Fan* quilt.

Dark fabrics

1. Using the template, cut 36 C quarter-circles.

Bright fabrics

1. Using the templates, cut 36 each of A and Ar
pieces and 72 each of B and Br pieces.

Background fabrics

1. Cut 18 squares, 8 x 8 inches in half diagonally
for the D background triangles.

Binding

1. Cut seven strips, 1 1/4 inches wide and seam
together to make a continuous length of 7 1/2 yards.

PUTTING THE BLOCKS TOGETHER

1. Following instructions for the Art Deco Fan
quilt, make 36 pieced blocks.

2. Divide the blocks into nine sets of four. Lay out
each group of four with the C quarter circles
together.

3. Sew the blocks together first in pairs. Press the
seams, then join pairs to complete nine large
blocks.

PUTTING THE QUILT TOGETHER

1. Arrange the blocks, then sew together into three
rows. Press seam allowances in opposite directions.
Join the rows together taking care to lock opposing
seams.

2. Using scrap fabrics, piece "crazy" borders in the
following dimensions:
two strips, 8 x 45 1/2 inches for the top and bottom;
two inner side border strips, 8 x 60 1/2 inches;

two outer side border strips, 4¹/₂ x 60¹/₂ inches. Piece the crazy patchwork by overlaying the folded edge of one piece on another and top-stitching using embroidery stitches.

3. Sew the crazy-pieced borders to the top and bottom, then the sides to complete the quilt top.

4. Press the quilt top carefully and remove any loose threads which may show through to the front.

5. Place the backing right side down on a flat surface. Center the batting then the quilt top over the backing, right side up. Baste the layers together thoroughly, starting from the center and working out diagonally, vertically and horizontally to the sides.

6. Quilt the fans ¹/₄ inch from their seams; add a simple grid between them, if required. Alternatively, quilt a motif in the centers of the large blocks. Tie the crazy patchwork borders using a square knot.

7. Use the Separate binding method to finish the raw edges of the quilt as described in the Techniques section.

WAVES

Repeating a single fabric in the border and the corner arcs of the
blocks provides a strong framework for this design. Skillful choice of
the right tones for the solid narrow arcs will be essential as well as
accurate sewing skills to maintain the regularity of the quilt.

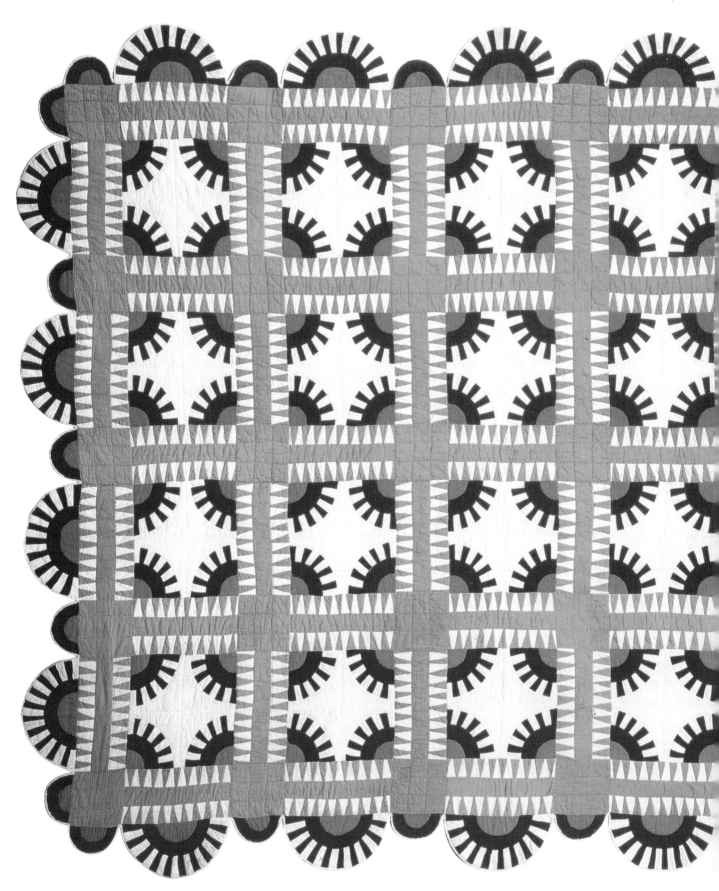

Art Deco New York Beauty

NEW YORK BEAUTY

Among the vast treasure house of
block patterns, New York Beauty was certain to
attract the eye of quiltmakers influenced by Art Deco
design. The sun ray motif expressed the optimism of a
forward-looking and modern culture.
New York Sunshine offers us a strong sun image seen
through a window-style grid, with recognizable panes.
The pattern's grid design resembles the steel structures
of the vast architectural development taking place
in American cities in the early part
of the twentieth century.

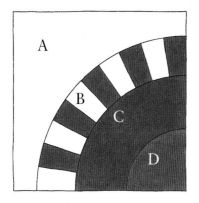

Skill level: Advanced
Quilt size: 80 x 96 inches
Finished block: 11 x 11 inches
Number of blocks: 20

MATERIALS

White 3³/4 yards
Green 4¹/4 yards
Red 2¹/4 yards
Orange ⁵/8 yard
Backing 6³/4 yards
Batting 84 x 100 inches, plus
   1 yard x 60 inches for the scalloped edges
Tracing paper for foundation paper piecing

CUTTING INSTRUCTIONS

Make templates for pieces A, C, D, LC, LD, SC and SD. The foundation paper piecing technique is used for the pieced arcs and the toothed setting strips, so templates are not required. Cut two lengths, 2³/4 yards for the backing fabric and set aside; the remaining fabric will be used for lining the scallops.

White fabric
1. Using the template, cut 80 block A backgrounds.

2. From the remaining fabric cut strips 1¹/4 inches wide for the pieced arcs. Begin by cutting a few strips, then more as required.

3. After the B arcs have been pieced, cut strips 1¹/2 inches wide for the pieced sashing strips. Cut a few strips, then more as required.

Green fabric
1. Cut 30 posts, 5³/4 x 5³/4 inches.

2. Cut 49 sashing strips, 2¹/4 x 11¹/2 inches.

3. From the remaining fabric, cut strips 1¹/2 inches wide for use in the pieced sashing strips. Cut more as required.

Red fabric
1. Using templates, cut 80 C arcs for the blocks, 18 LC arcs for the large scallops and 22 SC arcs for the small scallops.

2. From the remaining fabric, cut strips 1¹/4 inches wide for use in the pieced arcs, cutting more as required.

Orange fabric
1. Using the templates, cut 80 D corner pieces for the blocks, 18 LD semi-circles for the large scallops and 22 SD semi-circles for the small scallops.

PUTTING THE BLOCK TOGETHER

1. Trace four copies of arc B onto 6 inch squares of tracing paper. Mark ¹/4 inch seam allowances on all sides of the foundation.

2. Place a red strip on top of a white strip, right sides together, under a tracing, so that the first sewing line is parallel to the raw edges of the strips and ¼ inch away. Using a short 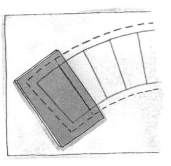 stitch length, sew along the drawn seam line, stitching to the seam allowances at both ends.

3. Turn over, open out the white strip and press lightly using a dry iron. Trim the strips. Folding the paper back from the stitching helps when trimming the fabric. Place the next red strip, right sides together, with the previous white strip so that its edge is parallel to, but ¼ inch beyond the next stitching line. Stitch on the line and across the seam allowances as before.

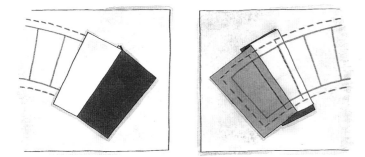

4. Open out the new red strip, press and trim. Complete the process to finish the arc. Make three more arcs on the remaining tracings. Press and trim the marked seam allowances but do not remove the papers. Set aside.

5. To join each red C arc and orange D corner piece, fold one of each in half lightly to find the center of the curved edges. Match the outer curve of the orange D corner piece to the inner curve of

the red C arc. Match the ends of the curves then insert pins at right angles across the seam at regular intervals, clipping the inside curve if necessary. Stitch 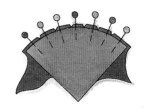 and press. Repeat to make four equal units.

6. In the same way, attach one unit to the inside curved edge of the red/white pieced B arcs. These units can now be sewn to the white block A backgrounds in the same way. Press and remove the papers. Sew these four units together to make the large block. Make a total of 20 blocks.

ASSEMBLING THE QUILT TOP

1. Work the red and white pieced arcs for the outer scallops over tracings of arc LB, using the method described above. Sew the orange and red semi-circles LC and LD together, then join to the pieced arcs. Make 18 of these.

2. To finish the scallop units, lay the pieced unit right side down onto strips of backing fabric over batting, cut 6 inches wide. Pin or baste. Machine carefully around the outer curve of the arc through all layers. Repeat for all arcs. Cut out leaving a scant ¼ inch seam allowance on the curved edge. Trim the batting close to the stitching. Clip the curves then turn right side out. Press the curved edges gently with the point of an iron. Baste the straight edges of each unit together and set aside.

3. In the same way, seam together the orange and red semi-circles SC and SD for the small scallop units. Make 22 of these units, then finish as in step 2

for the large scallops, but cutting the backing and batting strips 3¹/₄ inches wide.

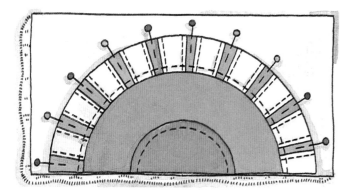

4. Quilt all the scallops in-the-ditch while they are separate and easier to manipulate.

5. To make the green and white pieced sashing strips, begin with two tracings per strip of the sawtooth design. Using the same foundation paper piecing method as for the pieced arcs, work the sawtooth strips using green and white fabrics. Note that on the original quilt not all the strips start and end identically. Make a total of 98 strips.

6. Make up the sashing strips by sewing a plain green strip 2¹/₄ x 11¹/₂ inches between two sawtooth strips. Trim the length of the strips to match. Make a total of 49 sashing strips.

7. On a flat surface, arrange the blocks, the assembled sashing strips and the posts using the quilt as a guide. Sew together in rows across the quilt, beginning with a row of green posts and sashing strips, then a row of sashing strips and blocks, and so on. Join the rows together matching the corners of the blocks and posts carefully.

8. Position the scallops around the sides putting the small scallops against the posts and the large scallops beside the sashing strips. Note that the scallops are very slightly smaller than the edge of the quilt that they sit beside. Turn each scallop over onto the quilt so that right sides are facing with raw edges even. Baste in place, then machine sew all around the outside of the quilt ¹/₄ inch from the edge to attach the scallops. After machining, baste the seam allowance to the wrong side of the quilt top, allowing the scallops to fall into place around the edges.

QUILTING & FINISHING

1. Divide the backing fabric into two equal lengths. Cut away the selvedges, then, with right sides together, sew a ¹/₂ inch seam down one long side. Press the seam to one side.

2. Assemble the quilt layers and baste thoroughly, starting at the center and working out to the quilt edges.

3. Quilt in-the-ditch around the arcs in the blocks and in the long seams of the sashing strips, continuing across the posts to simulate a nine-patch block. The quilt illustrated is also quilted in-the-ditch across the quarters of the large blocks, but a motif or simple grid can be substituted.

4. After quilting is completed, trim the batting level with the straight edges of the quilt, being careful not to cut into the scallops. Trim the backing to include ¹/₂ inch turnings. Fold the backing over to enclose the batting. Pin and baste the backing in place before stitching through all layers to finish.

NEW YORK SUNSHINE

Skill level: Advanced
Quilt size: 43$\frac{1}{2}$ x 38 inches
Finished block: 16 x 12 inches
Number of blocks: 4

MATERIALS

Blue 1¹/₂ yards
Yellow ¹/₂ yard
Garnet red 1¹/₄ yards
White 1 yard
Backing 1³/₈ yards
Batting 48 x 42 inches
Tracing paper for foundation paper piecing

CUTTING INSTRUCTIONS

Make templates for piece C. Add ¹/₄ inch seam allowances as you cut out each piece.

Blue fabric
1. Cut two strips for outer borders, 44 x 2 inches and one strip for the bottom border, 40 x 2 inches.

2. Cut two strips for the side inner borders, 37 x 3¹/₂ inches and two strips for top and bottom inner borders, 35 x 3¹/₂ inches.

3. Cut four background blocks, 16¹/₂ x 12¹/₂ inches.

Yellow fabric
1. Cut eight C corner pieces, using the template.

Garnet red fabric
1. Cut strips, 2 inches wide for the pieced B arcs. Begin by cutting a few strips, then more as required.

2. Cut four strips, 1¹/₄ inches wide, across the full width of the fabric. Join together to make a continuous length for binding.

White fabric
1. Cut strips 2 inches wide for working the pieced B arcs. As with the red fabric, cut more strips as required.

PUTTING THE BLOCKS TOGETHER

1. Make two tracings of arc B. Following the instructions for foundation paper piecing the arcs in *Art Deco New York Beauty*, and using the red and white 2 inch wide strips, work the pieced arcs. Press with a dry iron but do not remove the papers.

2. To insert the corner C pieces, find the center of the curved edge of piece C by lightly folding it in half, then match to the 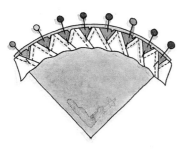 middle of the pieced arc, right sides together. Pin the ends of the arcs together and pin at right angles across the seams, clipping the inside curve as necessary. Sew. Repeat for the other corner unit.

3. Pin a pieced arc B onto one corner of a background block, then appliqué the curved edge to the background. Repeat with another corner unit on the diagonally opposite corner of the background block.

4. Make a total of four blocks. Trim away the background fabric from behind the appliquéd corner units.

PUTTING THE QUILT TOGETHER

1. For the pieced borders and sashing strips, foundation paper tracings are required. The finished width of all these strips is 1 inch, so draw out all strips with parallel lines 1 inch apart, then add $1/4$ inch seams on all sides of each tracing. Using these width dimensions, draw out the following foundation paper tracings: two strips, 41 inches for outer borders; one strip, 35 inches for the bottom border; three strips, 33 inchesfor the center sashing and inner borders; two strips, 27 inches long for top and bottom inner borders; and two strips, 12 inches long for horizontal sashing between the blocks. To mark the stitching lines for the pieced triangles, trace each strip from the template supplied. Start at the top of each strip and repeat until the required strip length is completely marked.

2. Piece the strips in the same way as the pieced arcs. After sewing, press each strip with a dry iron but do not remove the papers.

3. Using the quilt as a guide, lay out the four completed blocks with the pieced sashing strips. Pin, then sew the blocks to the sashing. Press, then sew the center sashing in between these units. Sew two pieced inner borders to the two long sides, and to the top and bottom.

4. Sew a blue inner border to the two long sides. Press and trim to size. Sew a blue inner border to the top and bottom, pressing and trimming as necessary.

5. Add two outer pieced borders to the two sides, then the final pieced border across the bottom.

6. Sew the blue outer borders first to the sides, press, then finally sew the remaining blue border to the bottom edge of the quilt.

7. Assemble the quilt layers and baste together thoroughly.

8. Echo quilt the pieced triangles $1/4$ inch away from the seam. Fill the remaining areas with a diagonal grid.

9. Trim away excess backing and batting. Bind using the prepared Separate binding.

NEW YORK TRELLIS

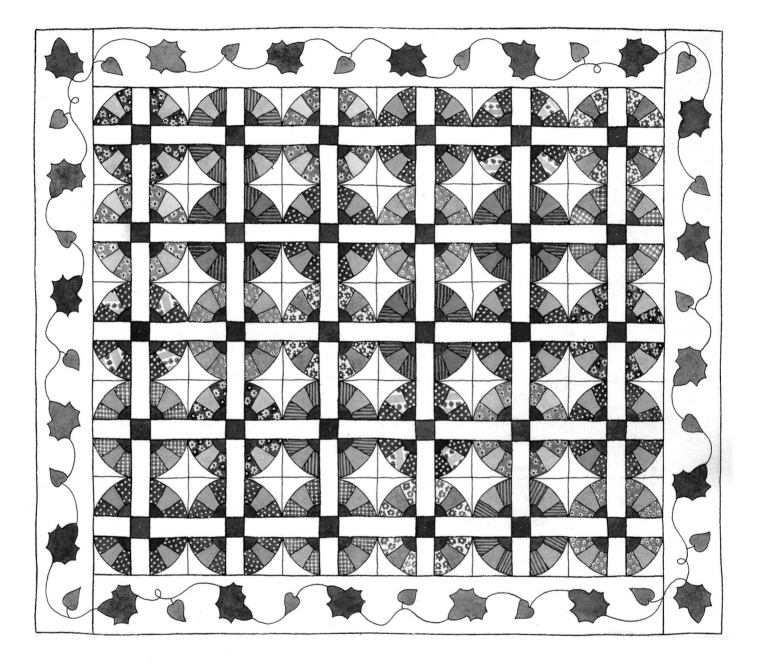

Skill level: Intermediate
Quilt size: 77¹/₂ x 90 inches
Finished block: 10 x 10 inches
Number of blocks: 20, 18 half blocks, 4 corner blocks

MATERIALS

White 4¹/₂ yards
Red ¹/₂ yard
Assorted red and blue prints equivalent to
3¹/₈ yards
Backing 5¹/₄ yards
Batting 81 x 94 inches
Binding 9¹/₂ yards
Embroidery thread for the vine stem

CUTTING INSTRUCTIONS

From the patterns provided, make templates for pieces A, B and C and for the border leaves. Add ¹/₄ inch seam allowances as you cut.

White fabric
1. Cut two border strips, 80 x 7³/₄ inches and two border strips, 77 x 7³/₄ inches wide.

2. Cut 49 sashing strips, 10¹/₂ x 3 inches and 22 sashing strips, 5¹/₂ x 3 inches.

3. Using the template, cut 120 block A backgrounds.

Red fabric
1. Cut 30 posts, 3 x 3 inches.

2. Using the template, cut 30 quarter-circles C.

Assorted red and blue prints
1. Using the template, cut B wedges for the pieced arcs. Where possible, cut sufficient fabric for four identical quarter blocks, i.e. cut eight wedges from one fabric and four wedges from another. Cut a total of 30 sets of wedges.

2. Cut 24 large leaves and 26-30 small leaves, using the templates supplied. Place the templates on the right side of the fabric and trace around them. Cut out adding a scant ¹/₄ inch seam allowance.

Binding
1. Cut a total of eight strips, 1¹/₄ inches across the full width of the assorted fabrics. Join together to make a continuous length of 9¹/₂ yards.

PUTTING THE BLOCKS TOGETHER

1. Work the quarter blocks units in sets of four. Sew the B wedges together in sets of three, two of the same print with a different one between.

2. To insert the red C quarter-circles, find the middle of the curved edge by folding it lightly in half and match to the center of the pieced arc.

Match and pin the ends then pin at right angles across the stitching line to ease the seams together, clipping the inside curve as necessary. Sew the seam carefully then press.

3. In a similar manner, attach the pieced arcs to the A pieces. Complete in sets of four quarter block units but do not join these together.

PUTTING THE QUILT TOGETHER

1. Using the quilt as a guide, arrange the blocks keeping the colors in the correct position. Pin, then sew two rows of quarter blocks and half blocks with short sashing strips in between. Label one for the first and one for the last horizontal row.

2. Assemble five pieced sashing strips by alternating five $10\frac{1}{2}$ inch sashing strips with red posts. Begin and end each pieced sashing strip with a $5\frac{1}{2}$ inch strip.

3. Using four quarter block units, piece four rows of five plates each. Begin and end each row with a

vertically set half-block and alternate blocks with sashing strips.

4. Sew the rows together in pairs then complete the central section of the quilt.

5. Appliqué the leaves to the white border strips, placing them freely. The stem, except for the ends, can be embroidered at this stage.

6. Attach the 80 inch borders to the top and bottom of the quilt. Press out, then add the 77 inch borders to the sides. Complete the appliqué and stem embroidery if required.

7. Assemble the quilt layers, baste together thoroughly, working from the center outwards, and quilt in-the-ditch around the quarter blocks, sashing strips, posts and leaves. The center A piece can be filled with echo quilting or a simple grid.

8. Trim the batting and backing to the edges of the quilt top and bind using the prepared Separate binding.

OPTICAL NEW YORK BEAUTY

Best described as a controlled scrap quilt, the organization
extends beyond the use of plain cream alternating blocks. Note the
four groups of 16 blocks each united by a consistent pairing of
shirting fabrics in the pieced arcs as well as the checkerboard
effect of the background fabrics.

TECHNIQUES

It is assumed that readers will have some knowledge of quiltmaking. However, many quilters are self-taught which often means that what they know depends upon their choice of projects in the past. The general advice contained within this section will help to fill any gaps and introduce some useful tips to quilters at all levels.

CHOICE OF FABRIC AND COLOR
Particular color combinations are associated with the Art Deco period and these will become apparent as you look through the quilts featured. The use of clear solid colors reminiscent of ceramics and enamels of the period, together with black, helps to set the period style. Dainty scattered and sprigged prints, both floral and geometric, so typical of the 1930s have recently enjoyed a revival of interest and reproductions of these prints will add the right flavor to any scrap quilt. The color scheme of a quilt can always be changed to suit your preference but before starting, make up a paper version of the block with the new palette clearly marked to avoid confusion as you start cutting.

PATTERNS
Some projects include actual size patterns; others for reasons of size have been reduced. The simplest method of enlarging is to make a photocopy enlargement, but make certain that your original is placed absolutely flat on the glass copy plate. This is essential to avoid distortion. Otherwise, to scale up the reduced patterns using the grid system, note the scale of the pattern, draw out a full scale grid of the correct-sized squares on an appropriately large sheet of paper. Copy the pattern onto the grid, square by square, by carefully drawing in the pattern lines within each square.

TEMPLATES
Template-making is not specified for all projects. In many cases, instructions are given for template-free cutting using the rotary cutting method. Before making templates, decide whether you will be piecing by hand or machine. Templates for hand-piecing are made without seam allowances, but those for machine-piecing include a $1/4$ inch seam allowance. Appliqué templates have no seam allowances added. After marking, a scant $1/4$ inch is added as you cut. Templates for blocks can be made by tracing the block design carefully onto light-weight paper. Cut the tracing apart and stick one of each component shape onto cardboard. More durable templates for large projects are best made from clear template plastic which can be placed directly over the original for marking. To avoid distortion, take care when making templates from photocopies for pieced blocks. Label templates accurately. Note that some shapes are labelled with an "r" after the main letter, e.g. Gr. This means that Template G must be flipped over and a given number of pieces cut in reverse. Having cut the templates, their accuracy can be checked by making a sample block from spare fabrics before proceeding to cut fabric for the whole project.

CUTTING OUT
Material requirements given are based on a careful use of 44 inch wide fabric but include a little extra to allow for the occasional mistake. In general, the largest pieces should be cut first and leftover fabric used for cutting smaller pieces. Except where stated otherwise, the sashing or border strip measurements will include about 2 inches for adjustment. Wherever practical, instructions are given for template-free cutting. For this method, the measurements always include a $1/4$ inch seam allowance. To cut a quantity of squares, for example, begin by cutting strips to the required size and then cross-cut to yield the correct number of squares.

Rotary Cutting
This speedy method of cutting requires three essential items - a transparent quilter's ruler, a rotary cutter and a self-healing cutting mat. The rotary cutter has a round blade which is very sharp and is shielded by a safety guard. It needs to be used with respect, both for your safety and to prolong its life. Always run the cutter way from you and remember to click the guard in place as soon as you have finished cutting. Having bought the equipment, it is worth investing time in practicing good cutting techniques. The following instructions are written for right-handed users. Left-handed quilters will reverse the instructions.

To prepare the fabric for cutting, it is necessary to

straighten and square off the crosswise grain - selvedge to selvedge across the width. Fold the fabric in half with the selvedges together, then fold again placing the second fold in line with the selvedges. Smooth the layers together and press, then place the fabric on the cutting board. Position the ruler on the fabric with one of the horizontal grid lines even with the double fold. It should be at the front of the board. Slide the ruler to the edge of the fabric, then press down firmly while you push the cutter along the edge of the ruler to make the first cut. Present the blade towards the edge of the ruler from the right until it touches the ruler, then bring the blade down to the mat. Holding it at a 45° angle, roll the cutter away from you so that the blade is turning as it reaches the fabric, and cuts right from the beginning of the fabric. Only a little downward pressure should be needed to cut a perfect strip. Up to eight layers can be cut with a sharp blade. By creating a 90° angle in the fabric as you cut, aligning a horizontal line on the ruler with the folded edges and the vertical edge of the ruler on the edges to be cut, you will ensure that the cut strips will be perfectly straight. After the edge has been straightened, fabric can be cut into strips, squares, rectangles and triangles by using either the grid on the board or on the ruler.

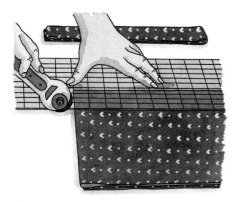

Cutting with Templates
When strip-cutting methods are not suitable, and templates need to be used, place templates for hand-piecing face down on the wrong side of the fabric. Trace around the shape with a sharp pencil. Leave at least 1/2 inch between pieces, and cut out adding 1/4 inch seam allowances all around. The pencil line is your stitching line. For appliqué, follow the same instructions as for hand-piecing, *but* place the template face up on the right side of the fabric. For both appliqué and hand-piecing, use finished size templates, which do not include seam allowances. For machine-piecing, templates include seam allowances. Place templates face down on the wrong side of the fabric, trace around the shapes, then cut out exactly along the pencil line. To conserve fabric and reduce cutting time, place adjacent templates next to each other so they share cutting lines.

PIECING TECHNIQUES
Hand-piecing

Lay the pieces right sides together, matching drawn seamlines. Begin with a backstitch, then sew along the pencil line with a running stitch. Take a backstitch at the end of the seam then finish off the thread. Do not sew across the seam allowances. When joining seams of pieced units, sew them together without stitching down the seam allowances by making a small backstitch just before the seam, passing the needle through the allowance, and making another backstitch before continuing to sew.

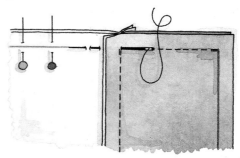

There are many blocks which require a piece to be set into a corner angle created by two other pieces. When the seam which creates the angle has been stitched, position the third piece along one edge of the angle and sew from the center point to the edge, keeping within the seam allowance on the marked lines. Pivot the patch through the angle and stitch along the second side again from the center outward. When joining pieces which meet at an angle other than a right angle, for example, diamonds and some triangles, offset the pieces so that the stitching lines, rather than the cut edges are aligned. Whether you choose to machine – or hand-piece, make sure you have joined the pieces correctly before adding the next piece.

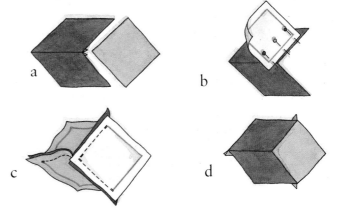

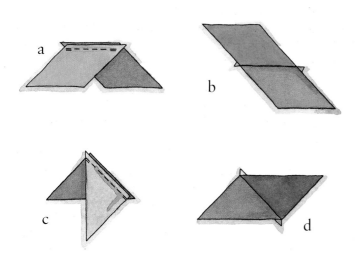

Machine-piecing

When machine-piecing, match the cut edges of the pieces and sew a straight, and accurate, 1/4 inch seam from edge to edge. Use the width of the machine presser foot as a guide, or adjust the sewing position of the needle so that it is exactly 1/4 inch from the cut edge of the fabric. Alternately, use layers of masking tape to mark a guideline 1/4 in to the right of the needle, on the throatplate of the machine. Seams are stitched from one edge across to the other, and pairs can be "chained-stitched" one after another, by feeding the pairs under the presser foot, without lifting it. Leave a stitch or two between each pair to prevent the stitching coming undone when cutting units apart.

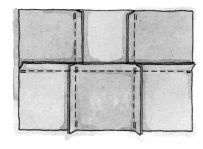

Press seams to one side, preferably towards the darker fabric. Always press seams before joining to the next unit. Where possible, press seams on adjoining rows in opposite directions so that the internal seams interlock when joining elements of a block, or rows of blocks together.

Foundation paper piecing

For some projects, foundation paper piecing is advised. This speeds up piecing certain designs and eliminates some of the time-consuming cutting of individual pieces. Using tracing paper or similar thin paper, make one tracing for each unit required on separate pieces of paper. All stitching is done by machine along the traced lines with the paper side uppermost, and using a short stitch length to facilitate later removal of the paper. Pin, or lightly fix with gluestick, a fabric piece large enough for the first patch in its correct position underneath the paper tracing. With right sides together, lay the second piece over the first, checking its position by holding it up to the light, if necessary, turning it over to check the finished position. Pin and turn over, paper side up. Machine along the drawn line, then turn, open out the second patch and fingerpress. Trim the seam allowance as appropriate. Repeat the process to add all subsequent pieces. Practice will reduce the need to turn over and check every piece before sewing. When units are complete, press and trim the sides to an accurate seam allowance ready for sewing to the adjoining pieces. After assembling, carefully tear away the foundation papers.

APPLIQUÉ

To prepare the cut pieces for appliqué, either fold the seam allowance to the wrong side exactly on the pencil line and baste under, or fingerpress seam allowances under using the edge of the template as a guide. Do not baste or turn under edges that will be covered by other appliquéd pieces. If the shape has deep valleys and sharp angles, you may need to clip into the seam allowance. Clip short of the pencil line to avoid fraying. When basting under sharp points, as in the border leaves of *New York Trellis*, trim away excess fabric from the point, fold down on the pencil line, then turn under the sides one at a time.

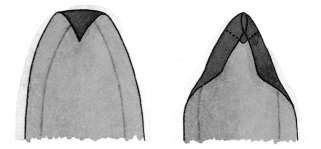

When appliquéing narrow bias stems, as in *Tiger Lilies* or *Stylized Vine Trails*, appliqué the inside curves to the background first, then stitch the outer curves. To prepare circles for appliqué, sew running stitches within the seam allowance, place a paper template in the center of the wrong side of the fabric circle and pull the thread to gather the circle around the template. Press carefully, using a light spray of starch to help set the shape. Remove the paper circle, then pin in position and slipstitch in place. Detailed illustrations of this technique accompany the *Dresden Plate* projects.

To help position the pieces on the background, fold the fabric in half diagonally, vertically and horizontally to give placement guidelines. Alternatively, place the background over a full-size pattern of the block and lightly trace around the design. To use this technique with dark background fabrics, you will need to place the block pattern and fabric over a light box for tracing.

Once your pieces are pinned or basted in position, stitch them to the background fabric working from the bottom to the top layer. For example, in the *Tiger Lilies* quilt, pin the prepared pink flower petals to the background, then tuck the yellow flower head under the concave edge. Using thread to match the color of the appliqué piece rather than the background fabric, slipstitch or blind hemstitch all around the shape. Then, appliqué the yellow center petal on top of the pink flower. When sewn correctly, you should only be able to see a tiny spot of thread on the front of the work. Do not pull stitches too tightly or they will pucker. Remove basting threads carefully when appliqué work is finished.

BORDERS

Most of the quilts featured in this collection have simple borders which balance and contain the central designs. Except where noted, all border measurements include an extra amount for trimming to fit. When fitting border strips to a quilt top, place pins at the center of each side of the quilt, and at the center of each border strip. Match centerpoints and pin border strips to the raw edges of the quilt, working from the center out to each corner, without stretching the edges. Stitch borders on using a standard 1/4 inch seam allowance and press.

With straight-cut borders, such as those used in *Scottie Dogs*, for example, the first two border strips are cut and sewn to the top and bottom edges of the quilt. The remaining borders for the sides must accommodate the additional width of the border pieces already attached.

Multiple borders, used in *Sunflowers*, *Pastel Wedding Rings* and *Fans-Pastel Crib Quilt*, combine two or three border strips for an effective frame to the central design. Strips are first joined together to make a pieced border strip, then applied to the quilt as a single unit. Corners can be straight, mitered or finished with corner posts. Another border option is a pieced border, as in *Blazing Star*, or *Crazy Fans*.

MARKING THE QUILT TOP

After the quilt top is complete, it must be marked with a quilting design. This should be done before the three quilt layers have been assembled. Use a well-sharpened hard lead pencil, artist's colored pencils, water-soluble felt tip fabric marker, or even a sliver of soap. Whatever marking method you use, it should be visible while you quilt, and be easily removed afterwards. It is advisable to test it first on a piece of scrap fabric.

Suggestions are given for suitable and typical quilting designs for each project. Quilting templates can be made by tracing the designs from the book directly onto template plastic and cutting out. Alternatively, trace the pattern with tracing paper, mount it on cardboard and cut out. Interior lines or channels must be cut out with a craft knife. Another method of transferring the quilting pattern is by tracing it directly onto the fabric. Tape a full-size pattern darkened with black marker underneath the fabric and trace. The design will show through light fabrics, but you may need to use a light box if marking onto dark fabric. Some designs do not require marking before assembling the layers together. These designs include: in-the-ditch, where the quilting is worked along the seam lines or immediately next to appliqué shapes; echo or outline quilting, where lines are stitched 1/4 inch away from seam lines and can be marked as you go with 1/4 inch masking tape; a simple grid can also be marked with masking tape; and motifs cut from sticky-backed plastic and positioned for stitching around.

ASSEMBLING THE QUILT TOP

After tidying loose ends and threads from the back of a completed quilt top, always give it a final press before assembling the layers. Do not press after the layers have been assembled. The heat from the iron may fuse the batting. Prepare the backing fabric, if necessary piecing to the required size. Press seam allowances to one side, and trim away selvedges. Tape the corners of the backing, face down, to a flat surface. Center the batting on top, smoothing out any wrinkles without stretching. Finally add the completed quilt top in the center, right sides up. If any repositioning is required, do not drag over the batting, but lift. Pin the layers together then baste thoroughly from the center outwards with large stitches. Ideally, you should baste in a grid with intersecting rows of stitches no more than 5 inches apart. For hand-quilting in a hoop or on the lap, basting needs to be closer than if working in a large frame. If planning to tie, the layers can be secured with safety pins – one every 4-6 inches. Take care to choose fine safety pins that will not stain or leave holes in the quilt.

QUILTING

Hand-quilting

Quilting stitches are small, even running stitches, which go through all three layers of the quilt, holding them together and adding a decorative texture to the quilt surface. The needle used for quilting is called a "between". Use size 8, 9 or 10 according to your preference.

Thread a needle with a length of quilting thread no longer than 18 inches and knot the end. With your basted quilt held taut in a quilting hoop and working from the center of the quilt towards the edges, insert the needle into the quilt top a small distance away from the point at which you plan to start. Tug the thread until the knot pops through and embeds itself in the batting. Use a thimble on the middle finger of the sewing hand, keeping the other hand underneath the work to guide the needle back up. Many quilters also use a thimble with a flattened top on a finger of the guiding hand which helps to push up the needle and protects the finger. Take three or four stitches with a rocking movement, keeping the thumb pressed down on the fabric just ahead of the stitching. Try to keep stitches as even as possible – this is more important than size. When the thread becomes too short, tie a knot close to the quilt surface and pop it through to the inner layers.

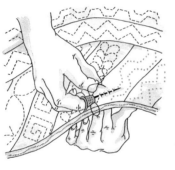

If you are having trouble "rocking" your needle in and out of the fabric, try loosening the tension of your quilting hoop. In order to quilt the outer edges of the quilt, baste strips of fabric approximately 9 inches wide down the sides of the quilt so that the hoop can be positioned correctly. Remove these strips, and basting stitches when quilting is complete.

Tying

Tying, also known as tufting, is an easy and economical technique of securing the quilt layers together. Using this method, the quilt is fastened at wide intervals — every 3 inches — so it is essential to use a polyester batting which will not shift. Thread a large-eyed needle with a length of pearl cotton, crochet cotton, or embroidery floss and stitch a backstitch over each point you wish to tie. Cut the thead leaving enough excess to tie a square knot in the ends, as illustrated in *Crazy Fans*.

BINDING AND FINISHING

Four common ways to finish the edges of a quilt are used within these projects.

Fold-finishing

After quilting, trim the top and backing to include $1/4$–$1/2$ inch turnings. Trim the batting to the finished size. Fold the backing to enclose the batting, and fold the seam allowance of the quilt top under so that it is even with the backing. Either stitch through all layers on the machine, slipstitch the folded edges together or sew together with a running stitch to match the quilting.

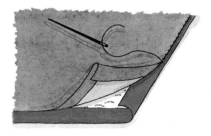

Self-binding

For this method, either the backing or the quilt top needs to be $3/4$–1 inch larger than the finished quilt size. If the backing is to be brought over to the front, choose fabric that complements the quilt top. Trim the quilt top and batting to the finished size and trim the backing to include the turnings mentioned above. Fold the backing over to the front, turn in the raw edge, pin and, if necessary, baste. Miter to keep the corners neat. Topstitch by machine, slipstitch, or blind hemstitch the folded edge to the quilt. If slip-stitching, it is advisable to add an extra quilting line just inside the binding to secure the batting. To bring the quilt top over to the back to self-bind, reverse these instructions.

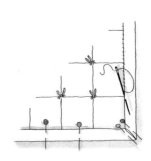

Straight Bind (Separate)
Though more time-consuming, straight binding gives a firm edge, wears well and offers a final opportunity to add a color statement to a quilt. Bindings can be single or double thickness. For single binding, cut sufficient strips of fabric 1¼ inches wide to equal the dimensions of the quilt plus about 10 inch extra. Join the strips with neat seams, pressing them open. Begin to attach the binding in the middle of one side, not at a corner. Place the binding on the right side of the quilt with right sides together. Fold over the beginning of the binding and pin in place down to the first corner. Stitch until exactly ¼ inch from the corner. Backstitch a short distance then remove from the work from the machine. Fold the binding up at an angle of 45°, then back down along the second side to be stitched. Pin and stitch, repeating the process to turn the remaining corners neatly. At the end,

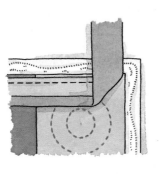
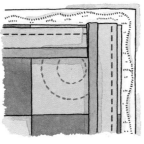
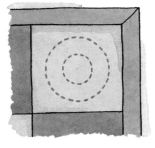

allow enough binding to overlap the start neatly and trim any excess. Fold the binding to the back of the quilt and hem in place along the line of machine stitching. Hand sew a few stitches to secure the miters at each corner. For double binding, cut strips 2½ inches wide. Press in half lengthwise, and pin to the quilt with raw edges matching. Proceed as for single binding.

Continuous Bias Binding
When the quilt has curved edges, the binding needs to be cut on the bias. The length of the bias strip obtained depends on the size of fabric used and the required width of binding. As a guide, a rectangle, 9 x 36 inch will make about 7 yards of bias, 1 inch wide, or about 5¼ yards of bias, 1¼ inch wide.

1. Start with as large a rectangle as can be cut from the fabric available. The exact proportions do not matter as long as the rectangle is true to the grain and has square corners. Press the fabric and place, right side down on a firm surface.

2. Find the true bias by folding one corner over so that the vertical side aligns with the bottom edge. Crease without stretching and cut along this line. Repeat at the opposite corner by folding it up so that the vertical aligns with the top edge. Again crease and cut.

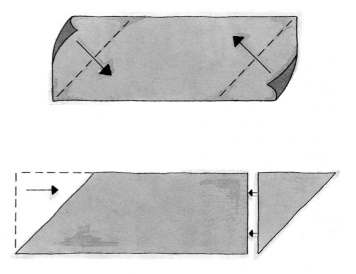

3. On the wrong side of the fabric draw parallel lines, the required width of the binding required, measuring at right angles from the first diagonal.

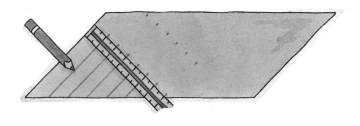

4. Along the top and bottom edges rule a line ¼ inch from the edge. These will be the stitching lines. Mark two points – A, at the top, left corner of the fabric and B, on the opposite side where the first ruled line meets the sewing line.

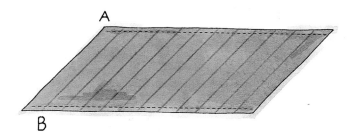

5. Insert a pin at Point A and, folding the fabric with right sides facing, pass the pin through Point B. Continue to match each of the lines on the top edge with the corresponding line on the opposite edge. At first, these edges do not seem to lie together but will eventually form into a spiralling seam around the fabric tube. The ends of the seams will be offset by the width of the bias strip.

6. Sew the seam along the marked sewing line using a short stitch length, about 20 stitches per 1 inch. Press the seam open.

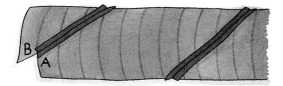

7. Beginning at the matched A and B points, cut around the spiral along the lines marked.

Apply the prepared continuous bias binding to the raw edges of the quilt following the same instructions as for straight binding.

TEMPLATES

PIECING AND APPLIQUÉ TEMPLATES

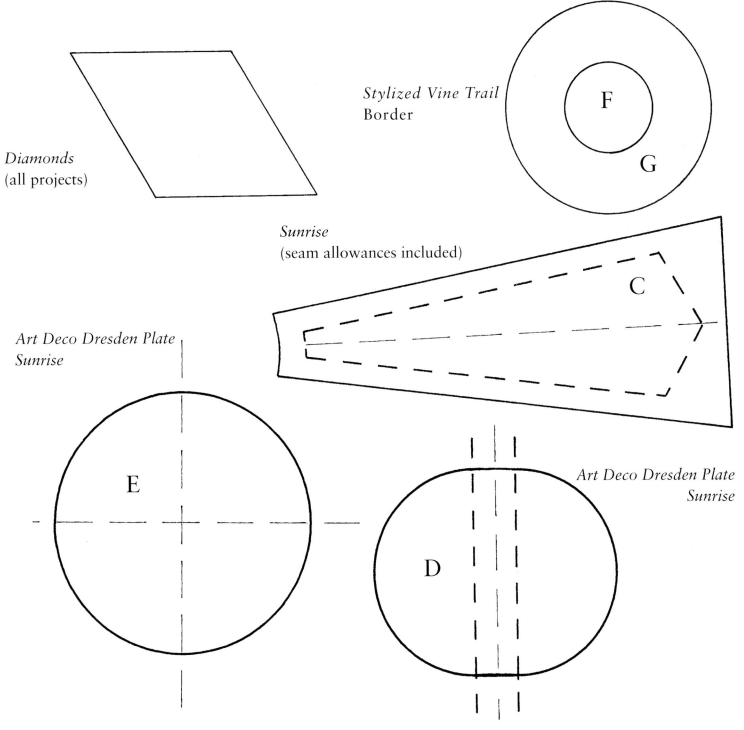

Stylized Vine Trail
Border

F

G

Diamonds
(all projects)

Sunrise
(seam allowances included)

C

Art Deco Dresden Plate
Sunrise

E

Art Deco Dresden Plate
Sunrise

D

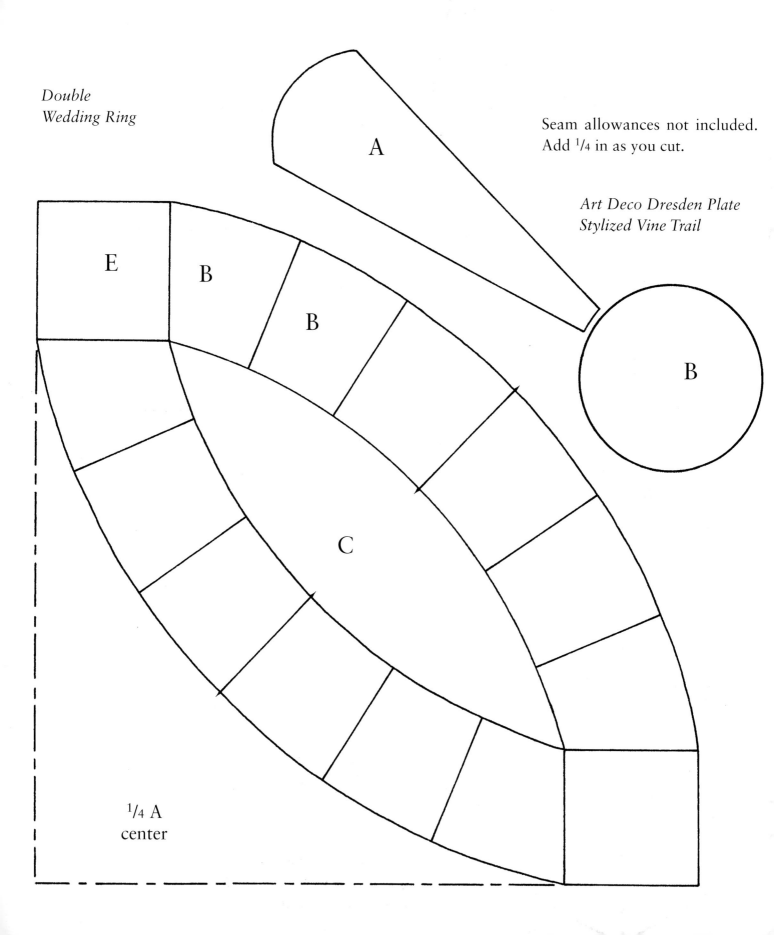

*Double
Wedding Ring*

Seam allowances not included.
Add ¹/₄ in as you cut.

*Art Deco Dresden Plate
Stylized Vine Trail*

A

E

B

B

B

C

¹/₄ A
center

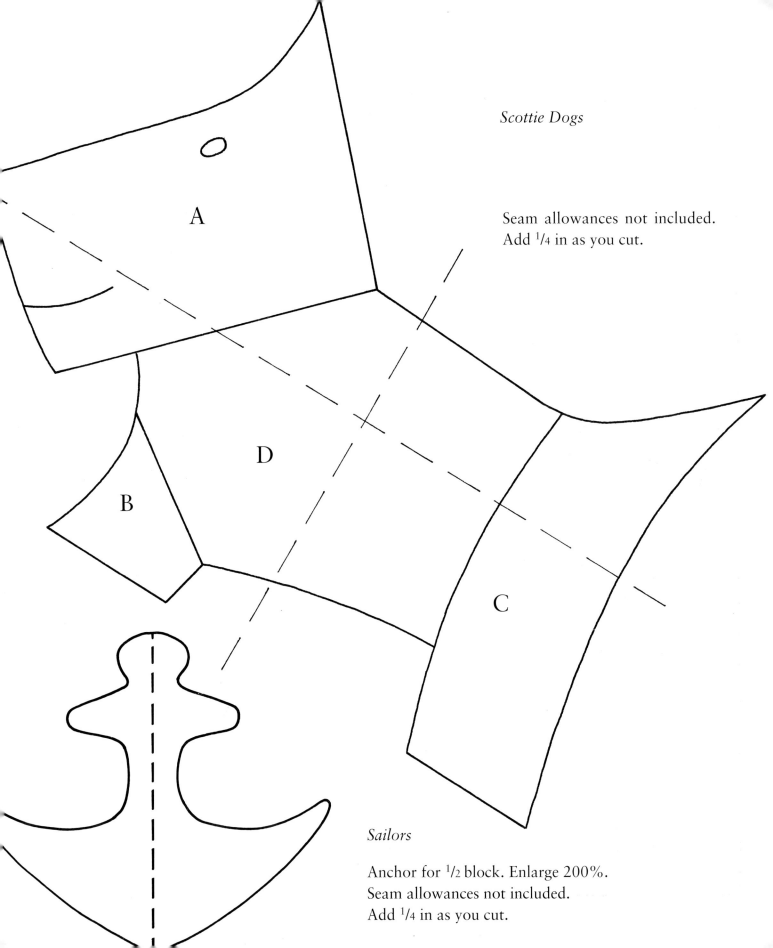

Scottie Dogs

Seam allowances not included.
Add $1/4$ in as you cut.

A

D

B

C

Sailors

Anchor for $1/2$ block. Enlarge 200%.
Seam allowances not included.
Add $1/4$ in as you cut.

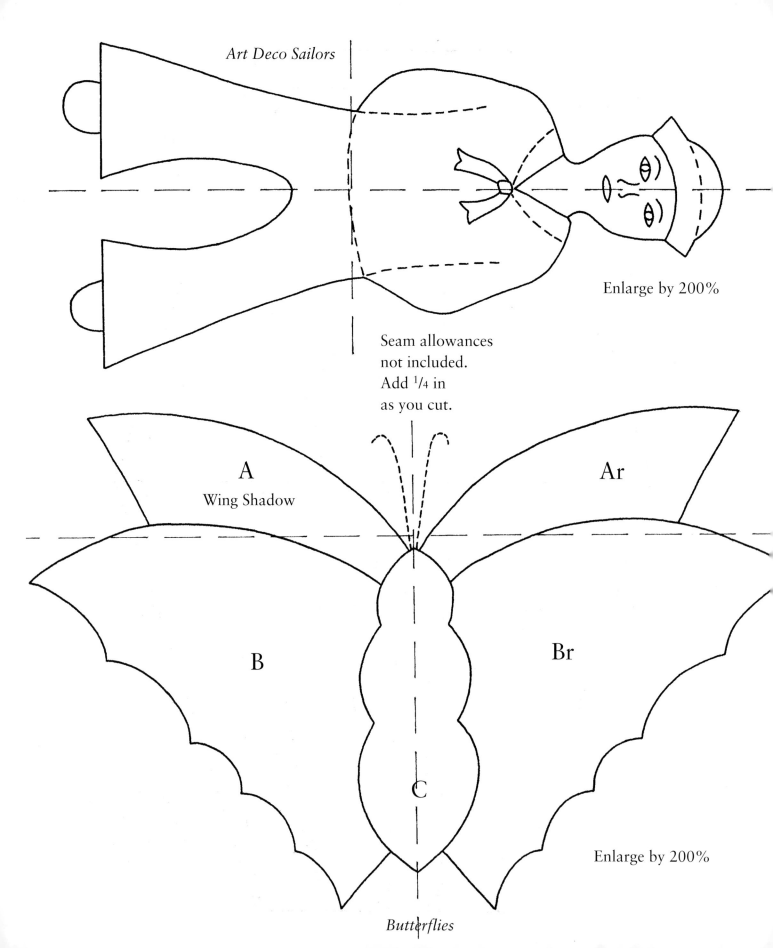

Art Deco Sailors

Enlarge by 200%

Seam allowances
not included.
Add ¹/₄ in
as you cut.

A
Wing Shadow

Ar

B

C

Br

Enlarge by 200%

Butterflies

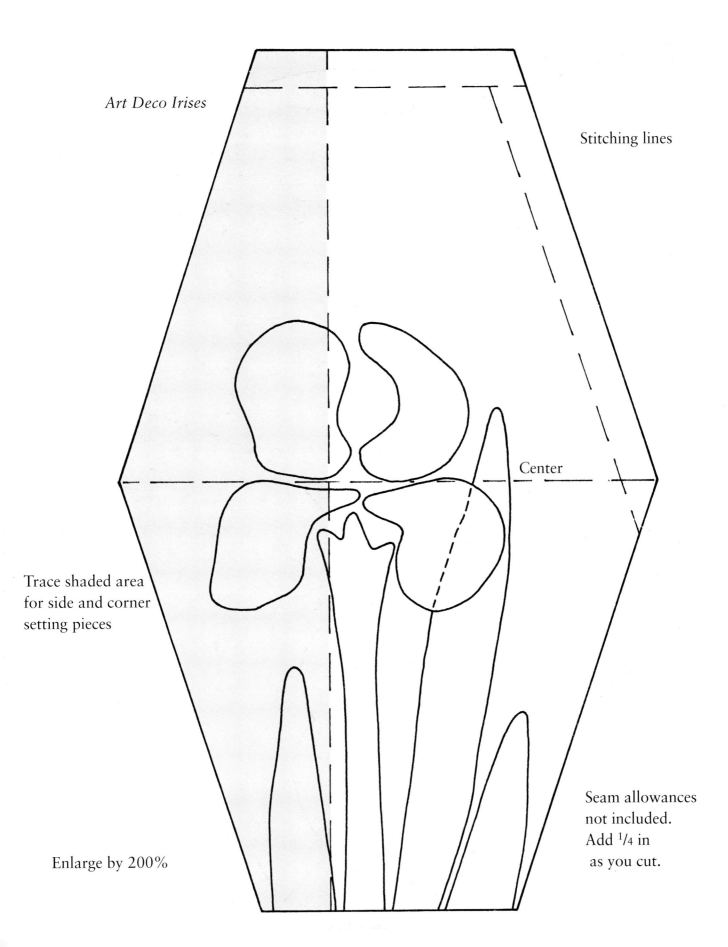

Art Deco Irises

Stitching lines

Center

Trace shaded area
for side and corner
setting pieces

Seam allowances
not included.
Add ¹/₄ in
as you cut.

Enlarge by 200%

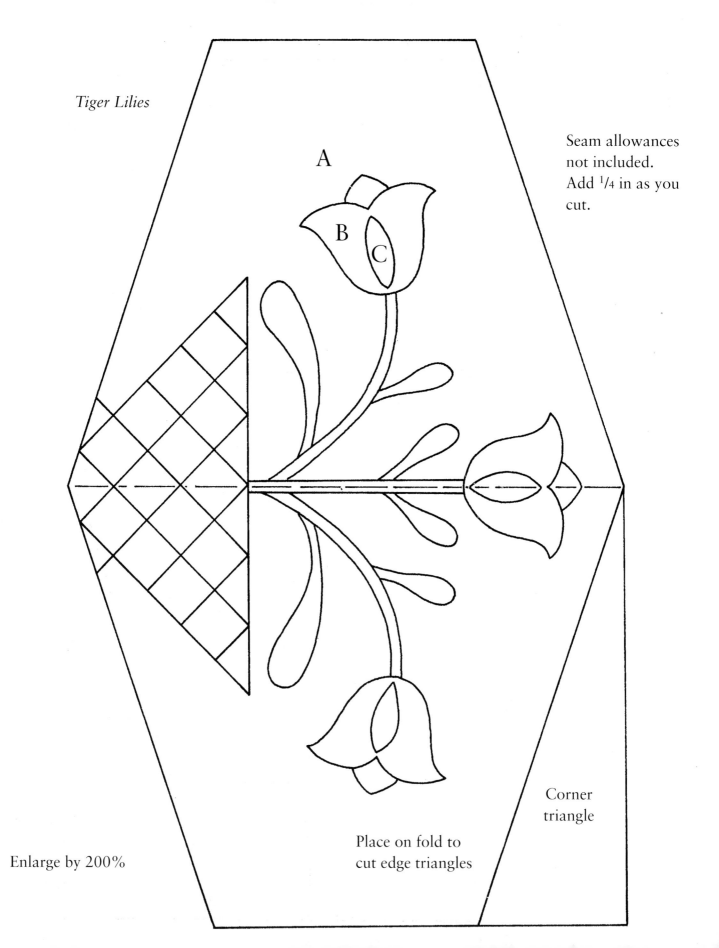

Tiger Lilies

A

B

C

Seam allowances
not included.
Add ¼ in as you
cut.

Corner
triangle

Place on fold to
cut edge triangles

Enlarge by 200%

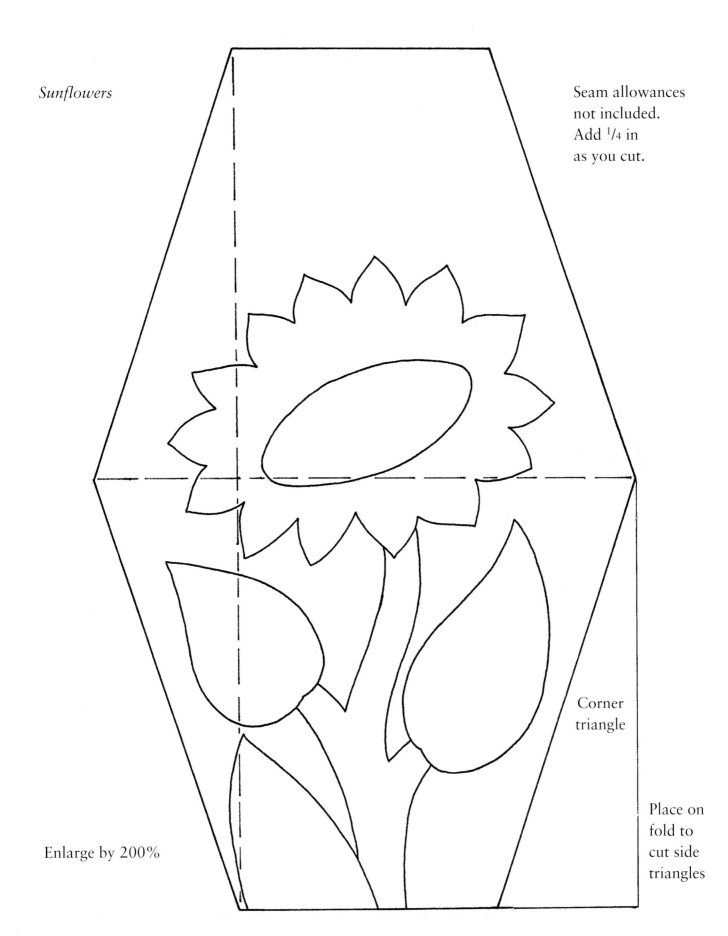

Sunflowers

Seam allowances
not included.
Add ¼ in
as you cut.

Corner
triangle

Place on
fold to
cut side
triangles

Enlarge by 200%

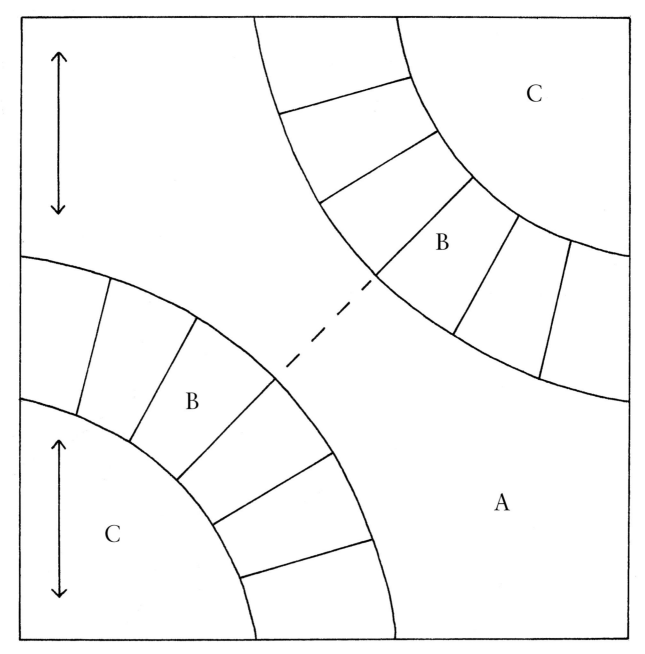

Snail Trails
(all projects)

Seam allowances not included.
Add $1/4$ in as you cut.

Seam allowances
not included.
Add $1/4$ in
 as you cut.

New York Trellis
$1/4$ BLOCK

New York Trellis border

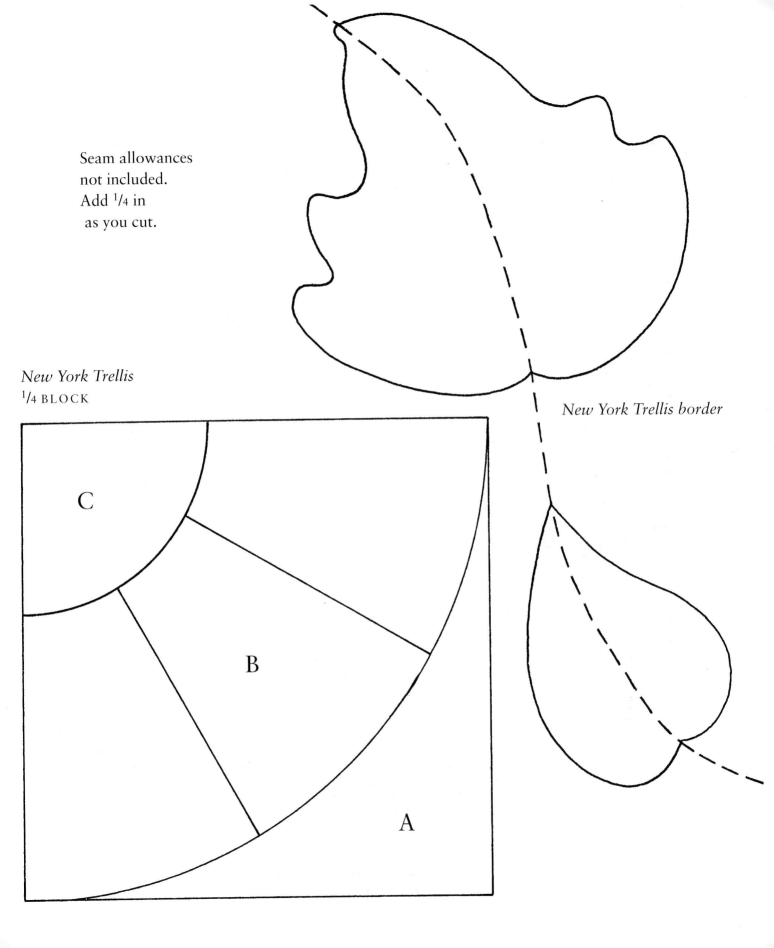

C

B

A

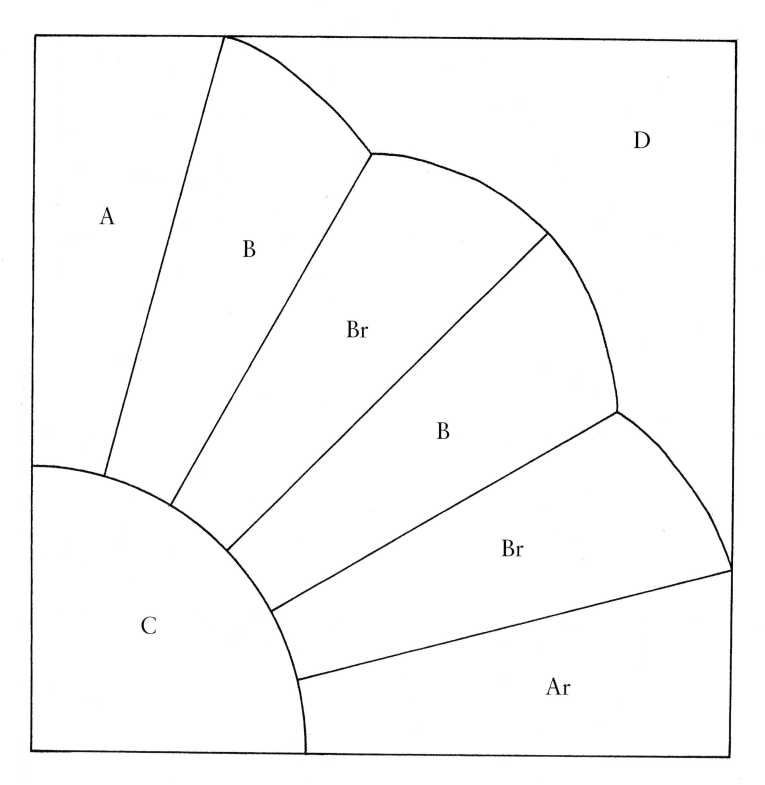

Seam allowances not included.
Add ¹/₄ in as you cut.

Fans
(all projects)

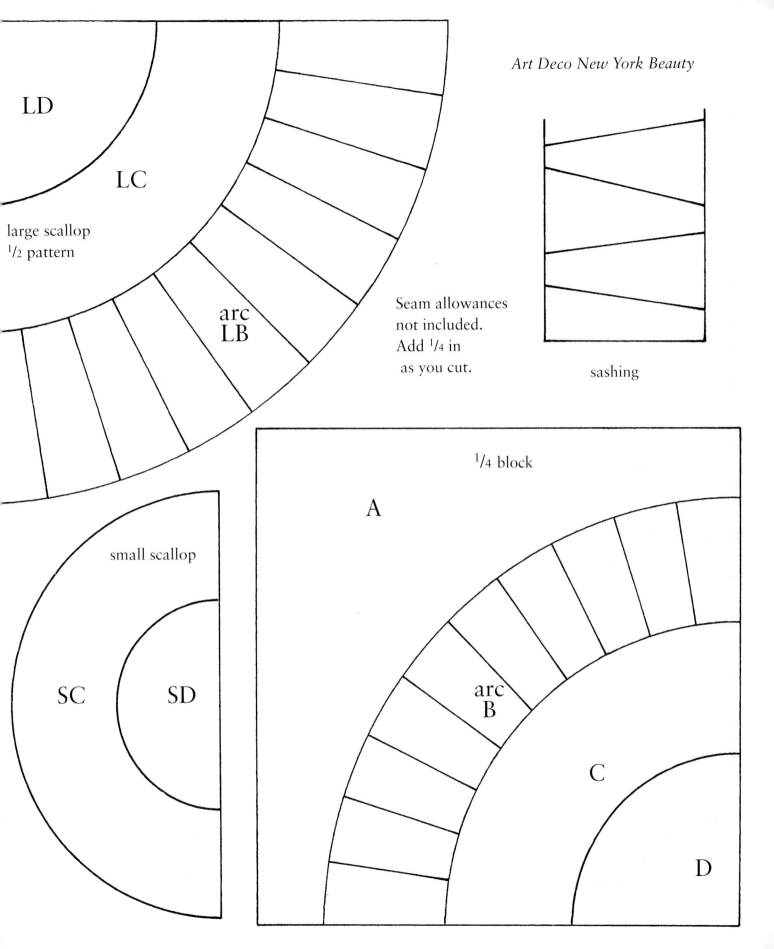

LD

LC

large scallop
$^1/_2$ pattern

arc
LB

Art Deco New York Beauty

Seam allowances
not included.
Add $^1/_4$ in
as you cut.

sashing

small scallop

SC

SD

$^1/_4$ block

A

arc
B

C

D

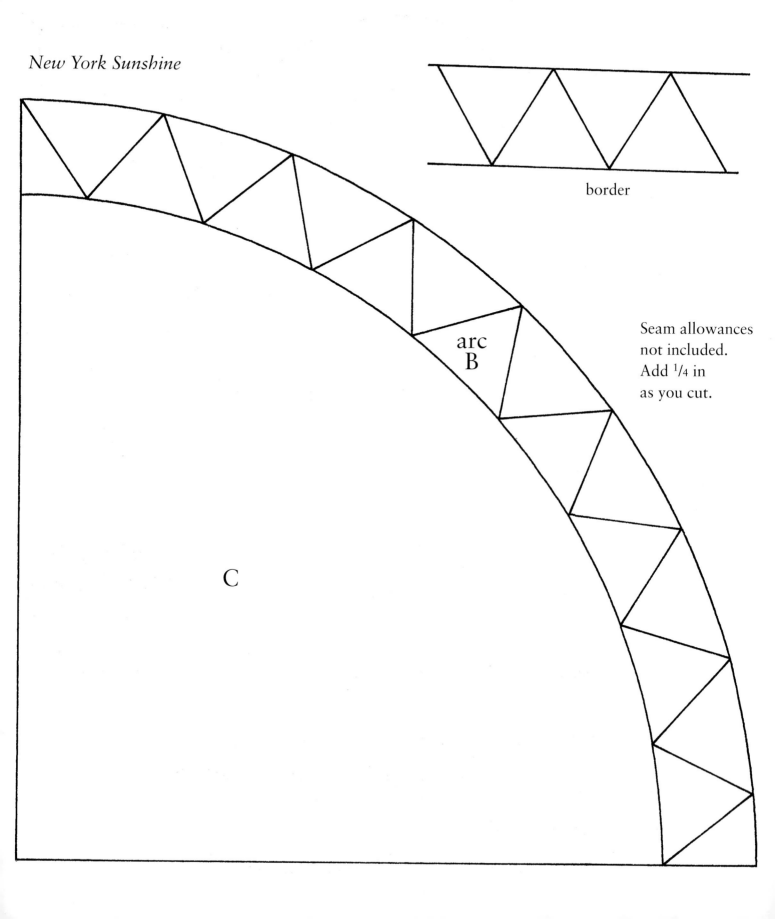

New York Sunshine

border

arc
B

C

Seam allowances
not included.
Add 1/4 in
as you cut.

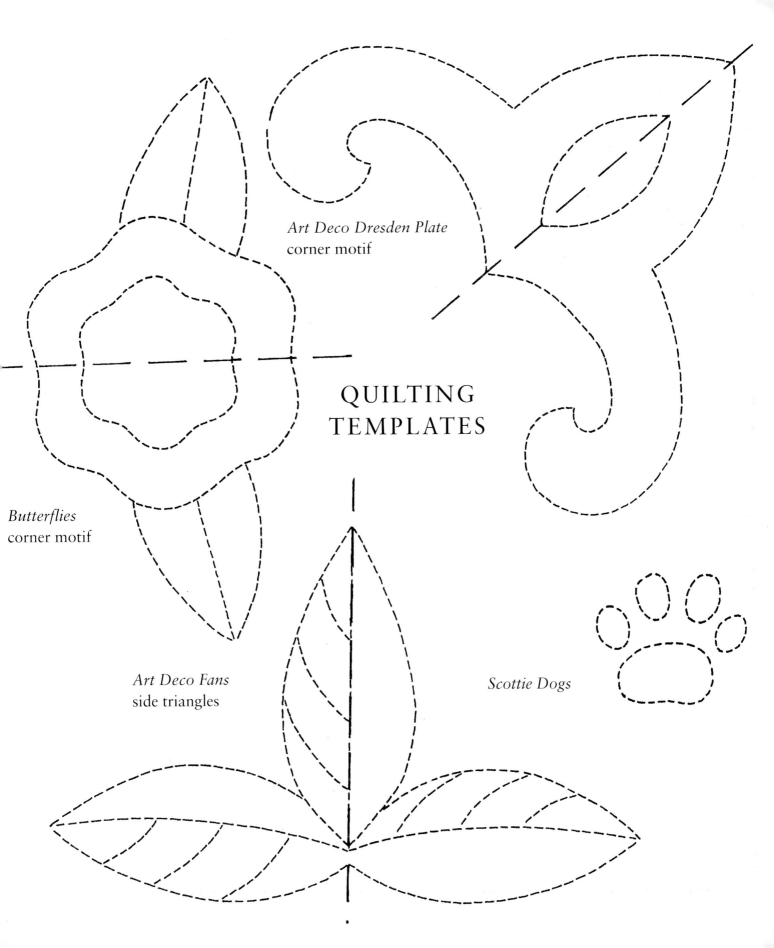

Art Deco Dresden Plate
corner motif

QUILTING
TEMPLATES

Butterflies
corner motif

Art Deco Fans
side triangles

Scottie Dogs

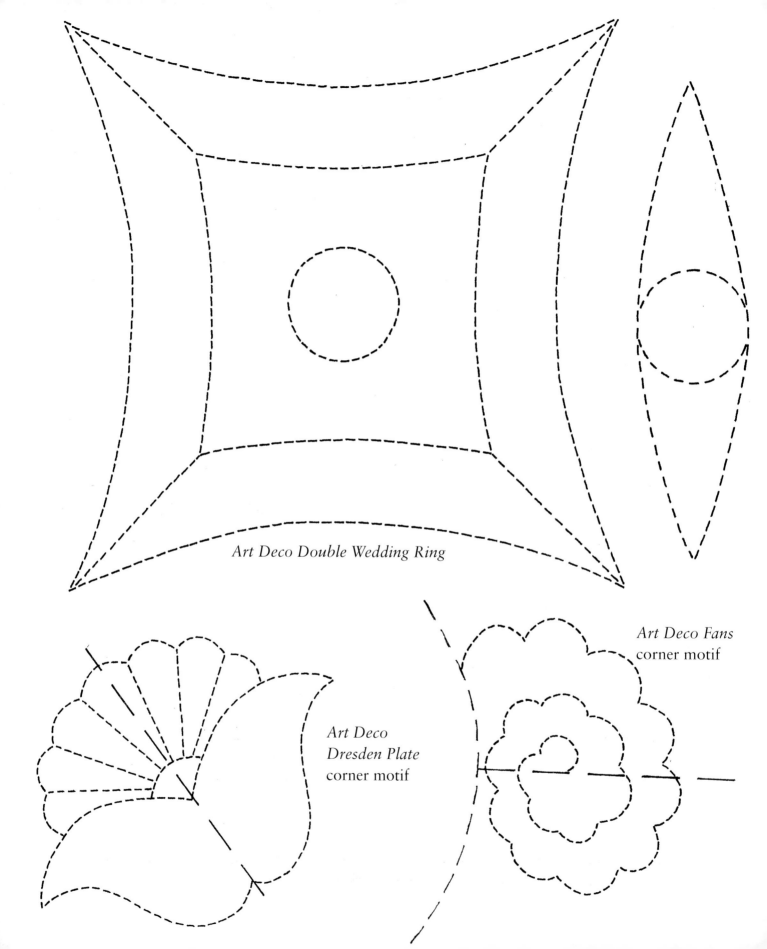

Art Deco Double Wedding Ring

Art Deco Fans corner motif

Art Deco Dresden Plate corner motif

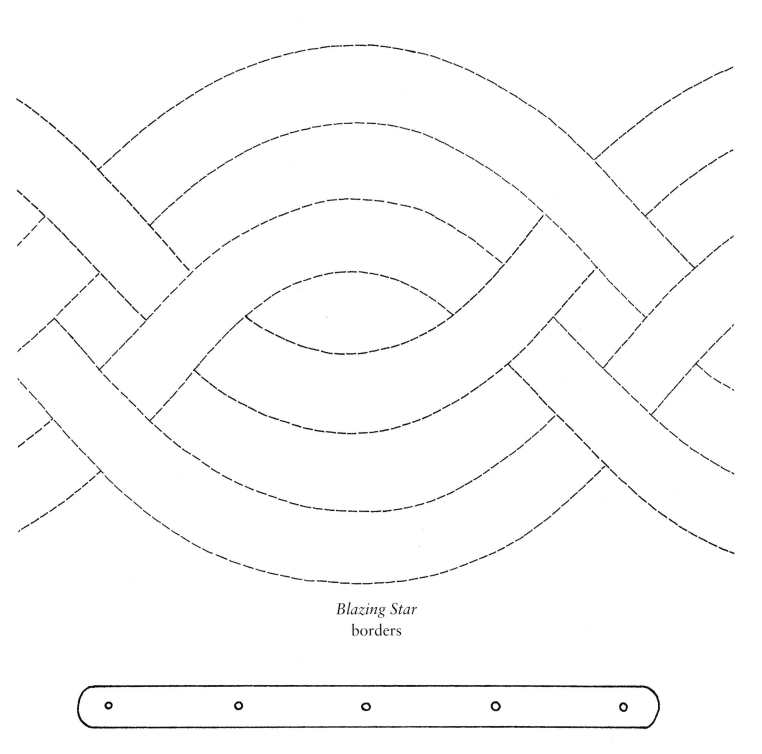

Blazing Star
borders

Snail Trails
Template for making concentric arcs.
Hold an end of the template at the corner of a block, insert the point of a pencil in a hole.
Swing the pencil to mark an even arc.

INDEX